Information and Documentation Resource Centres for Tourism

Guidelines for Establishment and Maintenance

Copyright © 2004 World Tourism Organization

Information and Documentation Resource Centres for Tourism
Guidelines for Establishment and Maintenance

ISBN: 92-844-0717-6

Published by the World Tourism Organization

All right reserved. No part of this book may be reproduced or transmitted in any form or by any means, electronic or mechanical, including photocopying, recording or by any information storage and retrieval system without permission from the World Tourism Organization.

The designations employed and the presentation of material in this publication do not imply the expression of any opinions whatsover on the part of the Secretariat of the World Tourism Organization concerning the legal status of any country, territory, city or area of its authorities or concerning the delimitation of its frontiers or boundaries.

Printed by the World Tourism Organization
Madrid, Spain

FOREWORD

One of the most significant characteristics of our time is undeniably the increasing importance of information as an instrument of socio-economic, technological and cultural progress on a global scale.

In the field of tourism as in other sectors, information is a crucial element for the short- medium- and long-term planning of this area of activity.

Public and private tourism actors are becoming more and more aware of the need to have qualitative and quantitative information at their disposal regarding the evolution of tourism activity and its outlook from the perspective of both supply and demand, as well as from the point of view of institutional measures that have an impact on its development at the national and international levels.

In this context, an information and documentation centre for tourism could serve as useful instrument for facilitating knowledge transfer by favouring the accumulation of information and its immediate availability.

Such an information management structure can thus effectively respond to the needs of different users, including tourism policymakers, by providing information that can help them formulate strategies for the sustainable development of the sector.

Aware of this situation, and in keeping with its goal of meeting the expectations of WTO Members in this area, the Secretariat of the Organization included the preparation of this Handbook on Setting Up and Running an Information and Documentation Resource Centre (IDRC) for the Tourism Sector as one of the programme activities for 2002-2003 under the heading of Documentation.

The present handbook was designed to address the needs of all those involved in information and documentation tasks and offers guidelines for establishing an information and documentation resource centre (IDRC) or a similar structure within administrations in charge of tourism. It consists of two parts. **Part one** discusses the basic elements needed to set up an IDRC as well as matters related to the function, administrative and material organization, activities, and computerization of such a centre. **Part two** is a veritable methodological and technical guide that shows the steps to be followed to establish and manage an IDRC, taking new information technologies into account.

With its transformation into a specialized agency of the United Nations, our Organization will be called upon to strengthen its development assistance actions in all the areas that fall under its competence.

With this in mind, the WTO will strive to enable all of its Members, particularly its Full Members, to benefit from the transfer of knowledge and know-how concerning the main aspects of tourism activity. This handbook on setting up and running an IDRC should thus make a significant contribution toward enhancing the capacity of tourism administrations to fully participate in the development of tourism information networking at the world level.

April 2004

Francesco Frangialli
Secretary-General of the
World Tourism Organization

ACKNOWLEDGEMENTS

The present Handbook on Setting Up and Running an Information and Documentation and Documentation Resource Centre (IDRC) for the Tourism Sector, was prepared under the responsibility of Patrice Tedjini, Chief of the Documentation Department of the World Tourism Organization (WTO) Secretariat. It was conceived and written by Mehrchid Minebachian-Berger, Head of the Information and Documentation Service of the France's Secretariat of State for Tourism, putting at the WTO's service twenty years of experience acquired through her current functions within the French national tourism administration, as well as through active participation in information and documentation engineering and training projects, both national and international. Adrienne Boncy, Assistant in the WTO Secretariat's Documentation Department, also contributed to the preparation and publication of this handbook.

TABLE OF CONTENTS

INTRODUCTION
　　Presentation 13
　　Objective 13
　　Methodology 13
　　How to use this handbook 15

I　GUIDELINES 17

I.1　Recommendations on the Role and the Function of an Information and Documentation Resource Centre (IDRC) Within a Tourism Administration 19
　　1.1　Role 19
　　1.2　Function 19
　　1.3　The Centre's coordination role and function at the national level . . . 20
　　1.4　Typology of documentation units possible within a Tourism Administration 21

I.2　The Administrative and Material Organisation of the IDRC 23
　　2.1　The IDRC's status and position in the organisation chart 23
　　2.2　The main administrative responsibilities 23
　　2.3　The qualifications of the Centre's staff 23
　　　　2.3.1　Recommendations on the job profile of the head of the centre: a director of documentary studies 24
　　　　2.3.2　Recommendations relating to the setting up of an IDRC's staff 24
　　　　2.3.3　The IDRC's staff: profiles and possible functions 25
　　2.4　Financing the Centre 28
　　　　2.4.1　The investment budget 29
　　　　2.4.2　The functioning of the budget 29
　　2.5　The organisation of office space, furniture and equipment 29
　　2.6　Identity record of an Information and Documentation Resource Centre as may be found in directories of information centres 31

I.3　The Main Activities of an Information and Documentation Resource Centre in the Field of Tourism 33
　　3.1　Traditional activities: the documentary sequence 33
　　3.2　New activities linked to the emergence of the information society and to new information and communication technologies 35
　　　　3.2.1　Economic intelligence 36
　　　　3.2.2　Collecting intelligence 37
　　　　3.2.3　Knowledge management 38
　　　　3.2.4　Records management 38
　　　　3.2.5　The activities of the Webmaster 39
　　　　3.2.6　Training and promotion 39

    3.3 A new process for managing information and documentation in the IDRC of the Tourist Authority (NTA) 40
          Documentation Mission Information Mission 42

I.4 Computerising the Document Holdings 43
    4.1 Planning the project 43
        4.1.1 Identifying the project.................................. 43
        4.1.2 The feasibility study 44
              4.1.2.1 An inventory of the Centre's holdings and services ... 44
              4.1.2.2 The description of the computerisation project 47
    4.2 Carrying out the project..................................... 49
        4.2.1 Drafting the job specification........................... 49
        4.2.2 The call of tender and the choice of the IT system 51
    4.3 Recommendations 52
        4.3.1 Choosing documentation software....................... 52
        4.3.2 Personnel training..................................... 52
        4.3.3 Product assistance and maintenance 53
        4.3.4 The creation of the databases 53
        4.3.5 Implementing computerisation standards................ 54

II METHODOLOGICAL & TECHNICAL GUIDE.................... 57

II.1 Identifying Demand 59
    1.1 A direct survey 59
    1.2 Indirect surveys 60
    1.3 The typology of information users 60
        1.3.1 Internal users... 60
        1.3.2 External users 61
    1.4 A permanent procedure for controlling and assessing users' satisfaction... 62
        1.4.1 Internal reques form 63
        1.4.2 External Request form................................. 64
        1.4.3 Visitor request form 65

II.2 Constituting the Document Holdings........................ 67
    2.1 What is a document?....................................... 67
    2.2 The typology of documents.................................. 68
    2.3 The specificity of tourism holdings 68
    2.4 The acquisition of documents 70
        2.4.1 Internal sources....................................... 70
        2.4.2 External sources...................................... 71
    2.5 The Centre's acquisition policy 72
        2.5.1 Acquiring documents.................................. 72
    2.6 The Documentation Charter / The Quality Charter............. 73

II.3 Classifying and Making an Inventory of the Document Holdings .. 75
    3.1 Accessioning. 75
    3.2 Shelf-marking documents 75
            3.2.1 Shelf-marking tourism holdings. 76
            3.2.2 A classification table for activities 79
    3.3 The preparation of the document. 80
    3.4 Making an inventory of the document holdings 81
    3.5 The list of statistics to be compiled and updated on an annual
         or monthly basis 81

II.4 Processing and Analysing Documents. 85
    4.1 The bibliographic description 85
    4.2 The abstract 88
    4.3 Indexing. 88
    4.4 The coding sheet. 89

II.5 Retrieving Information 93
    5.1 Information search with the help of the Thesaurus on
         Tourism & Leisure Activities. 93
    5.2 Exploring the Internet Network 96
            5.2.1 Basic steps for surfing the Internet 96
            5.2.2 Information retrieval and access strategies. 97
            5.2.3 Directories. 97
            5.2.4   Search engines 98
            5.2.5 Metamotors 98
            5.2.6 Intelligent agents and intelligence search on Internet. 99
            5.2.7 Internet directories for intelligence gathering 101

II.6 Creating and Distributing Documentary Products 103
    6.1 Files or dossiers 103
            6.1.1 Case files or documentary dossiers. 103
            6.1.2 Clipping files 103
            6.1.3 Dossiers on laws and regulations 103
    6.2 Lists, directories and compendiums. 104
            6.2.1 Directories or lists of tourism professionals. 104
            6.2.2 Compendium of legal texts. 106
    6.3 Technical sheets and methodological guides. 106
    6.4 Summary reports. 107
    6.5 Annual report 107
    6.6 Catalogues and bibliographies. 108
    6.7 Press reviews and press tables of contents reviews 109
    6.8 Electronic products 109
            6.8.1 Creating an Internet site 109
            6.8.2 The Intranet: a documentary information portal 110
            6.8.3 Intranet as a portal for the IDRC 111

II.7 Organising Intelligence Gathering....113
- 7.1 Building up an intelligence gathering network.....113
- 7.2 Creating the electronic newsletter.....114
  - 7.2.1 The layout.....114
  - 7.2.2 The contents of the newsletter.....114
  - 7.2.3 Internal and external Internet links.....116
- 7.3 Organising intelligence gathering within the IDRC.....116
- 7.4 Organising intelligence gathering on the Internet.....116
  - 7.4.1 Searching on the Internet.....116
  - 7.4.2 Creating a directory of sites to monitor.....117
  - 7.4.3 Automating the monitoring of sites using intelligent agents.....118
- 7.5 Collecting and organising information.....118
- 7.6 Assessing and checking information.....119
- 7.7 Handling information.....119
- 7.8 Entering information into databases.....119
- 7.9 Distributing the newsletter.....119
- 7.10 A reader questionnaire.....120
- 7.11 Gathering economic or competitive intelligence.....120

ANNEXES

ANNEX 1 Flow chart for organising intelligence gathering in the field of tourism.....121

ANNEX 2 English-French terminology glossary.....123

ANNEX 3 Professional organizations and specialised publishers.....127

BIBLIOGRAPHY OF SUGGESTED READING AND STANDARDS..129

LIST OF TABLES AND MODEL SHEETS

Typology of documentation units possible within a Tourism Administration ... 21

Definitions of some personnel functions, classified into A, B or C profiles, with descending level of skills ... 25

Identity record of an Information and Documentation Resource Centre as may be found in directories of information centres ... 31

Chart of the three traditional stages of the documentary sequence in the National Tourism Administration ... 33

Flow chart of the new management of information of an IDRC within a Tourism Administration ... 42

Table showing the composition of the document holdings and their development ... 45

A description of the procedures for processing documentation ... 46

A description of documentation services ... 46

A cost check list for the computerisation of the IDRC ... 51

Data entry form for the database of bibliographical references ... 53

Data entry form for the database of tourism professionals ... 54

Data entry form for the database of tourism laws and regulations ... 54

Model of an internal request form ... 63

Model of an external request form ... 64

Model of a visitor request form ... 65

Administrative directive for the deposit of documents ... 71

Model of a letter accompanying an order of a book or subscription ... 72

Model of a letter asking to receive a specimen copy of a periodical ... 73

The Documentation Charter / The Quality Charter ... 74

Model of an alphanumerical shelf-mark classification for an IDRC of a Tourism Administration ... 77

Model of a classification table of tourist activities ... 80

Example of a loan slip ... 81

A list of statistics to be compiled and updated on an annual or monthly basis . 81

Standard model for a catalogue entry ... 86

Model of a bibliographic description for monographs ... 87

Model of a bibliographic description for an article ... 87

Model of a coding sheet (and the data entry form) of a bibliographic reference for an IDRC on tourism ... 89

Flow chart for using a thesaurus ... 95

Model of a directory of tourism professionals ... 104

Model of a compendium of legal texts ... 106

Model of the annual report of a Tourism Administration's IDRC ... 107

Model for creating a directory of electronic addresses making up an Internet intelligence gathering network ... 113

Model of a directory of Internet addresses to be monitored for intelligence gathering on Internet ... 117

Flow chart for organising intelligence gathering in the field of tourism ... 121

INTRODUCTION

Presentation

The present **Handbook on Setting Up and Running an Information and Documentation Resource Centre (IDRC) for the Tourism Sector,** was prepared pursuant to resolution 432(XIV) adopted by the WTO General Assembly at its fourteenth session (Seoul, Republic of Korea/Osaka, Japan, 24-29 September 2001) relative to the execution of the Programme of Work of the Organization for the period 2002-2003 prepared by the Secretary-General. This handbook is included as a special activity in Part B (Documentation) of Section 8 (Communications and Documentation), under Heading 3 (Assistance to Members in documentation resource development and legislation).

Objective

This guide is written for anyone coming into contact with information and documentation professions, without having had previous training in information management techniques. It should help persons faced with the situation of having to organise, manage and even computerise document holdings, within a unit which is more or less well-endowed with resources. In no way does this guide seek to replace formal, technical training as a documentalist or information manager. Instead, it sets out to help those who do not have access to such training.

The handbook is designed to meet the needs of countries which are Members of the WTO. From this point of view, it seeks to provide the government ministry/department responsible for tourism with essential tools and general guidelines for setting up an Information and Documentation Resource Centre within a National Tourism Administration (NTA). The Centre should then be able to gather, process and disseminate qualitative technical information related to the tourism sector and its activities.

The handbook also aims to provide practices which allow tourism information activities to be standardised, by offering common tools for processing and disseminating information, that is to say common languages in terms of a thesaurus, a lexicon and recommendations relating to documentation software, common standards for data entry as well as the presentation of information. The use of such common tools and of new information technologies should facilitate the creation of a world, tourist information portal under the auspices of the WTO.

Methodology

The handbook is made up of two parts. The first part outlines the guidelines for the creation and computerisation of an Information and Documentation Resource Centre (IDRC), within a National Tourism Administration, and as defined by the WTO in 1985. These guidelines cover both the role as well as the status of such a Centre and its organisation, activities and computerisation. The second part, which is a real methodological and technical guide, examines systematically the various stages in creating an IDRC. Information sheets are available as models, for each of the steps taken, and may be used individually, as necessary. This methodological choice is based on two imperatives:

- the first takes into consideration the diversity of situations which exist across countries and the different levels to which documentation units/departments are developed, where indeed these exist;

- the second imperative takes into account the diversity of qualifications of the personnel of a Centre which may be more or less trained in documentation and information techniques.

These imperatives explain why the method chosen aims at progressing from the simplest techniques and practices for managing information (collection, processing, dissemination), to new, more sophisticated practices. These have emerged with the rise of the information society and include the use of Internet, economic intelligence gathering, and knowledge management, all of which are new professional activities that have enhanced and transformed the traditional techniques of processing information and documentation.

A detailed table of contents outlines this progressive process. A second table lists all references made to the model sheets and tables.

A French-English and English-French glossary of terminology was created progressively as the drafting of this guide was undertaken. It lists the choices made of English and French terms.

As for the bibliography, it provides suggested reading, rather than an exhaustive list of reference books and articles.

HOW TO USE THIS HANDBOOK

This handbook has two parts, each containing several chapters.

PART ONE, "GUIDELINES", consists of four chapters:

- **Chapter 1** gives recommendations regarding the role and function of an information and documentation resource centre (IDRC) within a tourism administration.

- **Chapter 2** deals with the administrative and material organisation of an IDRC.

- **Chapter 3** describes the main activities of an IDRC in the field of tourism.

- **Chapter 4** indicates the steps for computerising document holdings.

PART TWO, "METHODOLOGICAL AND TECHNICAL GUIDE", consists of seven chapters:

- **Chapter 1** indicates the methods for identifying IDRC users and determining their information needs.

- **Chapter 2** provides a typology of the documents that make up an IDRC's holdings and discusses the specific characteristics of tourism holdings.

- **Chapter 3** deals with techniques for accessioning, classifying and making an inventory of the documents collected by an IDRC.

- **Chapter 4** presents documentation processing and analysis techniques.

- **Chapter 5** shows the means for carrying out automated information retrieval with the aid of a thesaurus.

- **Chapter 6** enumerates the different documentary products that can be offered by an IDRC.

- **Chapter 7** discusses how to implement a permanent system for gathering tourism sector information and documentation.

I GUIDELINES

I.1 RECOMMENDATIONS ON THE ROLE AND THE FUNCTION OF AN INFORMATION AND DOCUMENTATION RESOURCE CENTRE (IDRC) WITHIN A TOURISM ADMINISTRATION

The generation and dissemination of information at the level of governmental departments requires a strategic plan based on a clear and precise policy. The plan should set out the guidelines of the main actions to be taken as well as the key objectives. The strategic plan should also allow the typology of the documentary structure(s) to be defined (see Section 1.4 "Typology of documentary structures").

1.1 Role

The IDRC is the main unit within a Tourism Administration which collects, processes, disseminates and exchanges scientific and technical information (STI[1]) relating directly or indirectly to tourism activities, at the national and international level.

1.2 Function

The functions of such a unit may be defined as follows:

- to collect, select and process documentation and information on tourism and related activities which are likely to meet the specific information needs of the various users of the Centre;

- to provide all forms of information that may be used by the Tourism Administration in its plans, programmes and other work;

- to act as an information centre for the various, national educational and training organisations specialised in tourism;

- to disseminate the information collected and processed, using publications such as: bibliographies, press reviews, case files, newsletters etc. which are aimed at meeting the needs of the various users of tourism information, both nationally and internationally;

- to allow users of the Centre to consult and borrow documents;

- to identify information of interest to the Centre's users which may be available in other documentation centres and units, both nationally and internationally, with the aim of procuring such information if necessary;

- to promote the exchange of information with other, similar documentation centres in the world, in particular using Information and Communication Technologies.

---

[1] Throughout this handbook, the term "information" is used to designate "scientific and technical information" as it is understood in the documentation sector, in contrast to the term's uses in journalism and information technology.

These functions can be carried out progressively according to the needs of the Centre's users, and the material and human resources available. To this end, the Centre should be provided with a structure that can evolve as its activities expand and as the services it supplies develop.

1.3 The Centre's coordination role and function at the national level

In some countries, several public and private organisations, which are directly or indirectly concerned by tourism, will collect, process and disseminate technical information on tourism. Under these circumstances, and if there is no national centre responsible for coordinating the work of the various existing document holdings, then it is likely that work will be duplicated and that activities in centres will overlap. Furthermore, documentation is likely to be dispersed, and this will lead to further problems for users as they seek to locate and obtain rapidly the information they need.

These problems have been solved in some countries by the National Tourism Administration (NTA), where it has given its documentation centre the responsibility for setting up a national tourism information system that draws together the various "documentation units" which are involved in collecting, processing and disseminating information useful to the tourist sector as a whole.

Such a national organisation for coordinating tourism information will have the following, key functions:

- to rationalise the collection and acquisition of documentation;

- to centralise the accessioning of documents and information by establishing a union catalogue;

- to harmonise and standardise the technical procedures for processing tourism information, especially by formulating basic, common vocabulary for analysing, searching for and disseminating information;

- to promote the circulation and exchange of information between the various information units integrated within the library network; and,

- to diversify the "documentary products" and information services that are likely to meet the needs of users.

Whatever its size (local, national or international), an Information and Documentation Resource Centre in the field of tourism must above all be:

- an information service specialised in the tourism sector,
- a resource centre promoting the best use of the knowledge and documents held by its parent organisation,
- a centre responsible for disseminating information to its network of correspondents,
- an organisation capable providing advice when necessary.

1.4 Typology of documentation units possible within a Tourism Administration[2]

TYPE OF UNIT	MISSIONS	STATUS OF PARENT ORGANISATION
Information and Documentation Resource Centre with: - an information service, - a documentation centre, - a library	to serve the National Tourism Administration and its partners in the specific field of tourism to preserve the Administration's documentary heritage and to make it available to outside readers	governmental department or directorate general of central government
Documentation Centre or documentation department	to provide services to the employees of a directorate general or a technical department	directorate general of central government or national technical department or devolved department
Documentation unit or in-house unit[3]	to provide services to the staff of a sub-directorate or a unit working with the "central" documentation centre	sub-directorate or bureau

---

[2] This typology is based on existing documentation unit within France's Ministry of Public Works.

[3] The documentary field covered by a small documentation unit is restricted, usually limited to specified legal, technical or geographical areas.

I.2 THE ADMINISTRATIVE AND MATERIAL ORGANISATION OF THE IDRC

2.1 The IDRC's status and position in the organisation chart

The status and position of the IDRC should be fixed and known to all concerned. It should be noted that the position of the IDRC within the National Tourism Administration will influence its activities. For these reasons, a legal document (decree or circular) may be used to fix the legal and administrative basis of the Centre as well as of its functions. However, in practice, the personnel and professional qualities of director of the Centre and its personnel are equally important in determining the status and prestige of the Centre.

It is difficult to situate the exact position of the IDRC in the organisation chart of the Tourism Administration for all countries. Nevertheless, there are undeniable advantages in the Centre being autonomous and accountable for its activities directly to the top management of the Tourism Administration.

> The Information and Documentation Resource Centre of the National Tourism Administration has a national remit. It has not only a horizontal responsibility within the Tourism Administration, but with the advent of the information society the IDRC may be called upon to carry out **economic intelligence, as well as the management of knowledge and competencies**. As a result, the Centre will have a direct relationship with the NTA.

The administrative structure of the IDRC should be set out in an organisation chart as soon as it has a staff of more than three or four. It is important to know who does what, who has responsibility for whom, and how the various members of the staff are linked.

2.2 The main administrative responsibilities

Defining needs: this may be done by the information manager(s). It involves determining the types of users of the IDRC and the types of services they require. The definition of needs is dealt with in greater detail in the second part of this handbook.

Defining the attributions of the Centre: this is the responsibility of the head of the Centre, and this responsibility involves planning, coordinating, managing and controlling the activities, having formulated a general programme for the Centre which states its personnel and budget needs.

2.3 The qualifications of the Centre's staff

The professional qualifications of the head of the Centre and of its personnel are of prime importance to its effectiveness. The "professional" personnel is charged with processing information and should be trained in the field of information and documentation (documentation engineering) as well as in the economic, geographical and sociological aspects of tourism.

The importance of having qualified staff and sufficient personnel for the proper functioning of the Centre should be stressed. All too often, documentation centres in public Tourism Administrations are run by inadequate staff, unable to carry out the necessary work. Similarly, the technical complexity of information processing has often been under-estimated, as poorly qualified staff are recruited, leading in turn to poor quality services and the conclusion that documentation work as a whole is not useful.

2.3.1 Recommendations on the job profile of the head of the centre: a director of documentary studies

The director of the Information and Documentation Resource Centre of a Tourism Administration should be an expert, with post-graduate qualifications, and skills in management or extensive knowledge of the tourism sector. His/her competencies cover expertise in the field of documentation and computer technologies, the organisational abilities needed to administer a documentation system, to carry out assessments, to manage the Centre's staff, to execute projects etc.

The Centre's director should be able to define the jobs in the Centre, recruit staff, allocate tasks, evaluate the work of the Centre and present its activities in an annual report. The director should analyse needs and carry out inventories of existing holdings depending on whether a Centre is to be created or transformed. He/she should identify the problems of the Centre, fix its objectives, choose an appropriate strategy or policy, obtain the means required to implement it, establish a plan set out in stages, achieve the Centre's objectives, and ensure the control and assessment of the plan.

The director must also set out the contract specifications for computerising the Centre and for creating documentary databases. He/she must establish standards for computerising the Centre and the retrieval languages to be used (thesauruses, lexicons, lists of indexation terms etc.), as well as the IT products of the Centre (electronic newsletters, Internet site, Intranet site etc.).

The Centre's director will also draw up the list of annual and/or monthly statistics that need to be kept. He/she will draft the documents presenting the Centre, relating to: access to holdings, the instruction guide for users, the documentation charter. (Models for such documents are given in Part II of this handbook.)

2.3.2 Recommendations relating to the setting up of an IDRC's staff

Apart from secretarial work and general documentation assistance, the Centre's staff is made up of two types of information manager. The first (higher education/university graduates) have skills to master and use documentation techniques, manage staff, organise tasks, identify and resolve problems. The second (high-school graduates) have the basic knowledge of the information manager's profession and can carry out simpler tasks, for which the qualified information managers can train them.

2.3.3 The IDRC's staff: profiles and possible functions

Definitions of some personnel functions, classified into A, B or C profiles, with descending level of skills[4]

PROFILE A

Administrator of an electronic information service

He/she ensures the overall consistency of the content of a computerised information documentation system, its evolution and architecture, its production, control and its promotion.

Coordinator of a library network

He/she ensures the coordination between documentation centres or structures (or persons) responsible for collecting data, and which together constitute a library network (be it general or specialist). In most cases, such a documentation network produces one or several electronic information services, at the regional, national or international level. The network coordinator organises the cooperation across the various parts of the network, either by distributing documentary resources or by distributing activities: the production, exploitation and dissemination of data (bibliographies, texts, multimedia) by defining and applying set procedures.

Librarian-information manager

He/she manages the Centre's holdings and makes available documents useful to the work of people seeking information or to potential users of the Centre. Such activity may be in response to specific requests or at the librarian-information manager's own initiative.

Information manager-report writer

He/she draws together documentation on a particular subject and writes up a summary of the information for the specific users of the Centre. The information manager-report writer may also draft documents aimed at making the use of documentation tools easier for internal and external users of the Centre. This person will also take part in publishing such information.

---

[4] This list of profiles has been selected from a typology of documentation professions established by France's ADBS (Association des professionnels de l'information et de la documentation) <http://www.adbs.fr>. It is also based on profile examples found in France's public administration.

Designer-manager of indexing languages

He/she will provide users (end users as well as information analysers and indexers), a specific language or vocabulary aimed at improving the relevance of the information and documentation system. This person manages and develops the indexing languages (thesaurus, lexicon, vocabulary).

Multimedia designer

The multimedia designer will transform an idea for a publication into an interactive, multimedia tool, that will be vocational, pedagogical etc. depending on the characteristics of the product's users. He/she will choose and structure the information presented, in order to allow for various ways of consulting the product. The product will then be packaged for use on various supports available in the market (diskettes, CDROMs etc.).

Information manager

He/she should be able to carry out all the functions of the documentation centre: making available to users or potential users (on demand or at his/her own initiative) documents, extracts or factual data that meets users' demands for information. To this end, the information manager should also obtain and keep up the holdings as well as appropriate research tools.

Audiovisual information manager

He/she develops, analyses, preserves and exploits holdings in audiovisual documents, animated or fixed images: photographs, sound recordings, video recordings, and films. These activities are analogous to those of a documentation generalist. The audiovisual information manager may have to create documentary systems such as image databases. Generally speaking, when audiovisual documents are produced by the Centre's organisation, the collection and management rights to use such images need not be acquired. The information manager will normally be working within a centre specialised in audiovisual documents, which in turn may or may not be integrated within a larger documentation resource centre.

Information manager-trainer

This is an information manager who can provide training to internal and external users of the organisation. This activity relates mainly to the search, processing and management of information, and aims at making the Centre's users autonomous.

Documentary database manager

The aim is to administer a particular type of electronic information service made up by documentary databases.

Knowledge manager

He/she helps develop the coherence in the way of accessing and transferring knowledge and know-how within the organisation, and ensures that acquired knowledge is fully used or developed. This person also participates in managing tools and instruments which facilitate the mobilisation of knowledge.

Records manager

This is a typical function which combines the management of the organisation's documents and archivist activities undertaken by an archivist-information manager. For this function, the management of documents is viewed from the perspective of preserving the corporate memory of the organisation and proof of its activities.

Manager of documentary resources

He/she directs and coordinates the unit responsible for managing the documentary resources of the organisation, as well as managing the Centre's personnel and coordinating its activities with other departments.

Intelligence information manager

He/she provides the decision-makers with information that is selected and processed concerning changes to the organisation's operating environment (technology, competition, economics, regulation etc.), to help the organisation better formulate its policies.

Webmaster

The webmaster is responsible for ensuring the technical and/or functional exploitation of a unit, which contributes to an electronic service using Internet technology.

PROFILE B

Public information officer

He/she provides the interface between the Centre's users and its information resources, by analysing and interpreting users' needs and selecting relevant information by legal means, and presenting it in an appropriate manner, usually as a bibliography.

Acquisitions officer

This person is responsible for enriching the document holdings. Drawing on his/her knowledge of suppliers and on the needs of users, he/she can put the Centre's acquisition budget to best use, purchasing varied documents or information supports that are necessary to carrying out the mission of the organisation. The job runs from identifying and evaluating suppliers to cataloguing acquisitions, drafting tenders, organising financing and monitoring deliveries etc.

Documentary producer manager

He/she develops products derived from primary and secondary information: directories, bibliographic bulletins, source catalogues, case files, press reviews, yearbooks.

Analyst-indexer

He/she is responsible for processing the content of documents, extracting textual, conceptual or factual data from documents, codifying it and formalising it with a view to enriching the database and creating a documentary product.

PROFILE C

Assistant information manager

As a member of the team, this person assists the information manager or other information and documentation professionals in the practical or repetitive tasks of processing and making documents available. He/she may also carry out the following functions: manage document acquisitions, manage collections, index documents, receive users and search for documents, assist in documentary production.

Documentation auxiliary or secretary

This person is responsible for carrying out tasks necessary and specific to managing the documentary system or structure: ensuring secretarial services for acquisitions, accessioning and circulation of periodicals, loans etc. To work well in this environment, the person must know the basic vocabulary of the profession thoroughly and be familiar with the work of colleagues.

2.4 Financing the Centre

It is important that the Centre has its own budget, which it manages independently from the general administration of the NTA. This provides the Centre with greater autonomy and control over its own activities. It is necessary to distinguish between the budget for running costs and for investment.

2.4.1 The investment budget

It is established for the creation or reorganisation of the Centre and includes initial, one-off expenditure for a number of years. Such expenditure covers:

- the premises,
- furniture and specialised material,
- the collections: acquisition of the basic document holdings,
- consulting costs, studies and training.

These expenses are important and must be carried, once and for all, by the NTA. They do not enter into the annual budget of the Centre.

2.4.2 The functioning of the budget

The budget is annual and covers both fixed and running costs. Apart from personnel costs, which are often borne directly by the Tourism Administration, the budget includes:

- information processing: increasing the holdings, documentary activities, binding etc.,
- supplies: office equipment and documentary materials,
- information technology costs: PCs, programmes, peripherals (scanner etc.),
- maintenance of material and equipment: maintenance contracts for software, photocopiers, printers etc.,
- outside services: publishing, sub-contracting, mailing etc.

2.5 The organisation of office space, furniture and equipment

It is impossible to make specific recommendations concerning the organisation of the IDRC's office space and equipment, as this depends exclusively on the importance of the Centre and the resources allocated to it. However, a few general rules may be recalled.

Managing a documentation centre involves:

- arranging, managing and maintaining the premises,

- selecting equipment and furniture adapted to its activities.

The IDRC of the NTA needs to have premises that are spacious and light, making it possible not just to receive visitors but also to present documents. The size and arrangement of the Centre's premises will depend on its objectives as well as its human, material and financial resources. However, in order to have sufficient space to store the holdings, about one third of the total space of the Centre should be reserved for shelving and other equipment, one third for space to receive visitors and one third for room for the information managers to work in. The floor of the premises must obviously be able to carry the weight of the holdings and the Centre's equipment and furniture. Its temperature should be kept constant (between 18 and 20°C), with a relative humidity of 55%. The premises should comply with national health and safety standards for public places. As a department which serves the whole Tourism Administration, the Centre should be accessible and clearly identifiable for potential users, with opening days and hours to the public properly posted.

The Centre will include various forms of materiel:

- IT equipment: personal computers with CDROM drives, printers, scanners, access to Internet and specialised databases, as well as specific documentation software, economic intelligence software, wordprocessing etc.

- Furniture for receiving visitors: tables and chairs and space for consulting holdings, a circulation desk, a photocopier, microfilm or microfiches projectors, faxes etc.

- Furniture to store and to present documentation: shelving, display shelves, filing cabinets for case files and clipping files, microfiche filing cabinets, video storage cupboards, loan-card files, cataloguing and inventory cabinets, a "kardex" (a file for accessioning periodicals and controlling their acquisition) etc.

- Furniture: the management of the holdings requires specialised storage furniture for documents and document stationery (self-adhesive plastic to protect covers, stickers for classification numbers, bar codes, book and review covers etc.).

2.6 Identity record of an Information and Documentation Resource Centre as may be found in directories of information centres

Name of the Centre	Address	Director	Contact
Year of creation	Administrative status : Department or Authority		
Mission			
Personnel employed by the Centre		Foreign languages spoken	
Users of the Centre	Types of users		Network of correspondents
Services provided by the Centre: reprography, loans etc.			Visiting procedure

Characteristic of the document holdings: areas and fields covered, the geographic coverage of the Centre.

Size of the document holdings:

- Books and documents
- Periodicals
- Audiovisual documents and CDROMs
- Maps, plans and brochures

Referencing systems

- Thesaurus
- Classification table
- Lexicon
- Directory

Documentary products

- Catalogue
- Press reviews and clipping files
- Bibliographies
- Case files

Electronic products
- Databases
- CDROMs
- Electronic newsletters
- Internet site
- Intranet site

Publications by the Centre

I.3 THE MAIN ACTIVITIES OF AN INFORMATION AND DOCUMENTATION RESOURCE CENTRE IN THE FIELD OF TOURISM

The role and functions of an Information and Documentation Resource Centre were defined in the first chapter of this handbook. It should be stressed, however, that the functions listed relate to activities which, apart from the traditional activities of a documentation centre, require that particular attention is given to tourism, especially for the following activities:

- defining the documentation policy of the Tourism Administration,

- managing acquisitions and the overall budget,

- preparing, following-up and distributing documentation products, in particular using information and communication technologies,

- organising the Centre's relations with its users,

- collecting, exploiting and fully using the grey literature produced by the NTA,

- contributing to the documentation and information networks of the Administration and partner organisations.

3.1 Traditional activities : the documentary sequence

Traditionally, the activities of the IDRC, whatever its specialisation, may be represented by the following documentary sequence:

Collecting information ➡ processing information ➡ disseminating information

The documentary sequence draws on "documentation techniques", in other words "the whole range of knowledge and know-how which makes it possible to act on the documentation system and on each of its components, to produce them, to shape them and to transform them in order to be able to meet every user's demand for information relevantly". This necessarily leads to the creation and provision of information products.

However, documentation activities are not solely technical, they also involve communication whose goals are pre-established (the search for information).[5]

The following chart shows the three, traditional stages of the documentary sequence in the National Tourism Administration:

---

[5] The relationship between documentation techniques and information sciences is dealt with by Hubert Fondin, in: Documentaliste-Science de l'information 2002, vol 39, n°3.

Collecting information →	Processing information →	Disseminating information
Local and regional tourism organisations	Management and analysis	Meeting demand by telephone, mail, email
Institutional organisations and trade associations	Recording	Receiving and assisting visitors
	Sorting	
International tourism organisations	Documentary analysis	Distributing documentation products to internal and external networks
Foreign tourism organisations (by country)	Indexation	
	Classification ↓	Publication in specialised tourism reviews
Pedagogical organisations (universities and research bodies)	**Documentation products**	Participation in tourist events (trade fairs and congresses)
Press and publishing	Catalogues	
	Information newsletters	
	Bibliographies	
	Study summaries	
	Press reviews	
	Case files	

This chart shows how the documentation function is organised around an information system which connects the producers and users of information.

The development of Internet and the New Economy (the Net Economy) have thoroughly transformed the documentation function. Indeed, Internet is an information system which makes it possible to accede to information and publish it without having to manage nor enrich it. The Internet user has access not only to a worldwide library, but also to search engines that facilitate access to it. As a new and powerful intermediary between users and information, Internet quickly appeared to be a threat to the documentary sequence and to the profession of information managers, who had previously been considered as the key intermediary between users and information.

In this new context, the job of the information manager must evolve rapidly and take on new competencies and practices.

3.2 New activities linked to the emergence of the information society and to new information and communication technologies

Since the 1990s, the emergence of an information society and the advent of Information and Communication Technologies (ICT) along with the explosion of demand for information have contributed to the rapid rise of the information industry. This industry brings together producers and distributors of specialised information. It impacts on ever more institutional and private actors who seek to control the information production cycle as the market internationalises. New professions have emerged within this competitive environment which modify and transform the traditional job of information managers, who have henceforth become document@lists.

According to Jean Michel[6], the document@list, faced with hundreds of billions of items of information available on Internet (3 billion visible pages, 600 billion invisible pages, 1 to 3 billion documents, and 7.5 million pages created every day), must:

- know how to authenticate and validate information sources,

- know how to map out new areas of documentation information and their access paths,

- be able to master the technical formats of documents and know how to manipulate digital documents in order to make them available to users,

- provide new methods for stocking and exploiting information taken from the Internet,

- master the language of ICT (push, pull etc.) and the new tools of information management (the use of robots and intelligent agents, meta-motors, off-line web browsers, etc.),

- be able to develop and produce new products and services (Intranet, extranet, Internet sites, electronic newsletters etc.) to disseminate information,

- to sensitise and train users in the functioning of Internet,

- to organise new information access networks (directories of bookmarks/favorites, the presentation of sites by subjects, discussion groups, forums etc.)

---

[6] Michel, Jean: "Information et documentation, des métiers à redéfinir", in Problèmes économiques, No 2690, 29 November 2000.

3.2.1 Economic intelligence

Economic intelligence covers all activities related to gathering information about an organisation's competitive environment. "It includes all strategies for processing and using information for ensuring the permanence and the development of a company". It mobilises joint methods and means of communication to enrich the strategic knowledge of the company and to transform its capacity.

The aim is to identify, process, interpret and disseminate information with the object of clarifying decisions and favouring forward-looking behaviour.

According to Jean-Louis Levet[7] today's global transformation is not so much that of the information society, but rather the shift from the information society to the "knowledge society". Economies are no longer based on labour and the production of material goods but on knowledge, in other words education, training and research.

Economic intelligence is the combination of management tools such as gathering intelligence about an organisation's environment, benchmarking[8], providing information (producing value added at the precise moment that decisions are made), and knowledge management.

As a result, economic intelligence is a system which fulfils four essential functions: mastery of knowledge and know-how; the identification and understanding of opportunities, risks and threats (risks being the obsolescence of a company's or an organisation's knowledge and know-how, threats relating more to an attack on the image of the a company or an organisation); the coordination of actors and activities in order to favour collective learning and develop the habit of sharing information; the development of strategies to influence its environment upstream.

France Bouthillier[9], a Canadian academic, distinguishes six stages that characterise the collection of intelligence:

- Identifying information needs,
- Acquiring information,
- Organising, preserving and locating information,
- Analysing information,

---

[7] Jean-Louis Levet is Head of Technological and Industrial Development at the French Planning Agency. He is also President of the French Association for the Development of Economic Intelligence.

[8] This term originated in marketing and refers to the process of rigorous and systematic assessment which companies make of their environment.

[9] This process was put forward by France Bouthillier at a conference on economic intelligence organised at the IDT/Net 2002 trade, and was published in Bases, No183, May 2002.

- Developing intelligence products,

- Distributing intelligence.

3.2.2 Collecting intelligence

According to AFNOR (the French official body for establishing product standards) "collecting intelligence is an on-going, largely interactive activity which aims at surveying an organisation's technological and commercial environment etc. in order to anticipate change in this environment". Carrying out such intelligence collection involves observing and analysing the environment surrounding the activity in question. It is a key component of economic intelligence in general, and should feed into the strategic decision-making process. Companies and States acting in the competitive, global market are constantly forced into developing their strategic position, or safeguarding it. This explains why they collect intelligence, which may be carried out by a single person or by a group of experts (strategic group, intelligence group etc.).

Documentation centres and information managers may participate actively and fully in these groups and in these new activities (collect, analyse, organise and disseminate). Technically speaking, collecting intelligence follows the more conventional documentary sequence. Various forms of intelligence collection may be identified:

- technological intelligence relates to the search for and exploitation of scientific and technical information as well as information related to technology (production procedures, materials etc.);

- competitive intelligence collection is carried out in direct contact with the top management of the government department or company and seeks to generate information about actual and potential competitors;

- commercial intelligence concerns more clients and suppliers of a company, products and market trends;

- legal intelligence relates to legislation and regulations affecting a particular sector;

- geopolitical intelligence deals with the international environment, as well as political and social risks of countries under study;

- economic intelligence coordinates all the other forms of seeking intelligence and provides input into the decision-making process of the department/organisation concerned.

3.2.3 Knowledge management

This activity involves capitalising on an organisation's knowledge and know-how and sharing these within a network. Sharing knowledge involves drawing it together within a community of experts, processing it, making best use of it and disseminating it back within the community or to other collaborators, independently of their real geographical location. Knowledge management involves the direct exchange of information by:

- creating directories of experts which identify experts and their key areas of competence, and hence mapping out available knowledge;

- facilitating the work of networks by training professionals and experts concerned in the use of IT tools (databases, Intranet, forums etc.) so that they may exchange their information about a project or on a particular theme;

- Coordinating communities by bringing together people with similar professional interests, through meetings, working groups etc.

3.2.4 Records management

According to ISO 15-489[10] (April 2002), records management is the "field of organisation and management for the effective and systematic control of the creation, reception, preservation, use and destination of documents, including methods for fixing and preserving evidence and information related to the nature of the documents". In other words, records management consists in the preservation of documents concerning an organisation or company, its functions, policies, decisions and actions.

"The purpose of records management is to make information available in the right place, at the right time, at the lowest cost. Records management controls official records from the time they are created or received until they are either destroyed or archived."[11]

"Arising first in the United States at the end of the 19th century, records management comprises a set of methods and techniques aimed at organising the efficient management of documents within the organisation in which they are produced, from their creation until they are deposited in archives. The procedures involved in 'records management', which range from registering documents to the ways in which they are ultimately stored or eliminated, have gone through various autonomous changes, mainly in English-speaking countries in which these procedures are applied". Organically linked to the structure which carries out "records management", the activity has also evolved differently in companies and public administrations [...]. Where archivists develop these concepts, "records management" consists of more

---

[10] The second part of this standard (NF ISO 15489-2) sets out the methodology for implementing the standard, in manual format which recommends the various aspects of "records management" and defines the results to be expected.

[11] Records Management Programme, Office of Administration, U.S. Small Business Administration, December 1998.

modest, yet also more pragmatic, tools adapted to each working context and geared to allowing an organisation to know fully what information it actually contains".[12] (It should be noted that at the time of publication of this handbook, the English term "records management" had not yet been suitably translated into French.)

The major outlines of records management and its application to the preservation of documents generated by a National Tourism Administration will be set out in the second part of this handbook, in the chapter on document classification.

3.2.5 The activities of the Webmaster

Being able to organise and manage an Internet site or web pages related to information and documentation is part of a Centre's duties, as is designing and creating an Intranet which meets the requirements of an organisation's departments. The second part of this guide will deal with the creation of Intranet and Internet sites in greater detail.

3.2.6 Training and promotion

The spread of new technology means that information managers need to be increasingly pedagogical in their work and may even be called on to organise training and self-training for the users of an IDRC. Such training mainly involves providing IT support, training users in the use of Internet, the effective use of search engines, documentary databases, indexing languages, Boolean operators etc.

The interest of the IDRC's users can be maintained by promoting Internet and Intranet sites as well as by organising events: the presentation of studies, thematic conferences, the presentation of pedagogical instruments, open-days.

All these new techniques and activities may now be considered to be part of the functions of a documentation centre and may be set out in the objectives of the IDRC of the NTA.

Tourism is a multidisciplinary activity in which professionals and experts from different fields work: economics, sociology, business and commerce, statistics, culture, heritage, the environment etc. This makes it all the more important to apply the principles of knowledge management. Similarly, competition among countries and destinations receiving tourists is increasingly organised at the global level, as the leading countries seek to maintain their rankings. They have increasing recourse to economic intelligence gathering to help formulate national policies. Collecting economic intelligence is therefore organised along the lines of the major areas of tourism, such as sustainable development, the preservation of natural and cultural heritage under threat from industrial pollution, or natural catastrophes. As a result,

---

12 "Comment le records management peut faire progresser la transparence administrative", communication given by Philippe Barbat, Directorate for Archives, France, 2001.

economic and business intelligence groups have been set up in major tourist destinations.

This handbook has sought to take into account this context and the specific factors that stem from it, which explains why the manual recommends the application of up-to-date knowledge management techniques and structures within the Tourism Administration.

3.3 A new process for managing information and documentation in the IDRC of the NTA

This process functions in three stages

Stage I – Evaluating demand, both internal and external, by the use of a qualitative and quantitative system of analysis which makes it possible to identify and anticipate the needs of internal and external users. The second part of this handbook presents the various ways of carrying out such a survey.

Stage II – Creating the document holdings by setting up a system for capitalising information available and for referencing information.

The system of capitalisation is based on collecting and generating three types of data and documents:

- the knowledge and know-how of the agents of the NTA, which need to be determined using the method of knowledge management described above, and which are subsequently entered into a database set up to this end;

- public and private-sector data available on tourism: i.e. all publications and reports produced by the Tourism Administration, professional organisations, institutions and educational organisms etc. Such data should be analysed and entered into the bibliographical database. The data is indexed and may be digitised with electronic document management programmes, which allow the full text of documents to be stored.

- an inventory of the living memory of the NTA, based on all forms of documents which present the creation and the evolution of the Administration, its organisation, the status of its personnel, the policy orientations of successive ministers, laws drafted by the Administration's departments and other legislation affecting the organisation of tourism in the country. All such documents should be preserved in full text, within the databases.

The referencing system consists of selecting or creating tools that permit the wealth of stored data to be accessed and exploited. This involves mainly creating lexicons, thesauruses, classification systems, glossaries of technical terms or vocabulary relating to information technologies. These tools are necessary to index or classify documents and to facilitate the search for information within the databases. The aim is also to create tools that facilitate the search for information on Internet, such as thematic directories of Internet sites, directories of intelligent agents, electronic directories and electronic mailing lists.

Stage III – Disseminating information by formulating and coordinating information systems

It is necessary not just to determine the most efficient means for meeting demands made of the Tourism Administration, but also to be capable of anticipating needs, by creating information tools accessible to everyone. This requires setting up an Internet site available to an external public, which not only indicates publications produced by the NTA, but also data, special reports and bibliographical databases. The setting up of Intranet or extranet sites is reserved for meeting the needs of the staff of the Tourism Administration and/or its regional offices.

Coordinating and promoting the use of such a system requires the staff of the NTA to be trained and encouraged to use the technology available to them. It is also necessary to capture and hold the attention of outside users, by sending them newsletters covering economic intelligence gathering, and any other information related to tourism. By continually analysing the demand for information, the staff of the IDRC can ensure that its work is updated and enriched.

The following flow chart sets out these three stages of managing information, stipulating for each stage the methodologies and techniques applied, as well as the competencies employed by a document@list.

The three stages overlap with the documentation sequence, reviewed and enriched by the use of new technology.

The Management of Information Within a Tourism Administration
A Three - Stage Mission

Stage I
Assessing internal and external demand
By using a qualitative and quantitative system which makes it possible to anticipate the needs of internal and external users.

Stage II

Documentation Mission

	System of capitalisation		Referencing system	
Capitalisation of the knowledge and know-how of the Authority	Capitalisation of public and private data on tourism	Capitalisation and enrichment of the living memory of the Authority	Developing technical referencing tools and languages	Creating shared tools

Stage III

Information Mission

Developing information systems		Managing information systems	
Internet, Intranet, Extranet		Publication of economic and business intelligence products	Training staff

Applied methodologies and techniques

| Knowledge management | Permanent inventory systems: data collection, management, cataloguing, digitising for database storage | Study of the evolution of the history, organisation and public policy of tourism | Thesauruses, lexicons, classification plans, terminology sheets relating to ICT | Thematic directories of Internet sites, directories of intelligent agents, electronic directories, mailing lists | Developing the architecture and contents in order to meet demand / Enriching, publishing and promoting public data on tourism | Developing newsletters, using economic intelligence and web-watching | Motivating and encouraging the use of ICT and research on Internet |

Skills to be applied

| Knowledge management | Documentation techniques and documentary information, database management | Knowledge of organisation (records management), its foundation and legal evolution | Knowledge of linguistics, terminology applied to and on tourism, "Internet culture" | Knowledge of needs within the sector | Documentation sciences, concise knowledge of the theory and techniques of communication and IT culture | Knowledge of strategic intelligence, electronic publishing and IT | Promotion and training |

I.4 COMPUTERISING THE DOCUMENT HOLDINGS

In the late 1980s, it was still possible to ask whether it was worth computerising a documentation centre, a library or an archive. It was then necessary to carry out (either internally or by an outside service provider) a cost-benefit analysis of the project, and to convince the finance department of the organisation. In the Age of Internet and the Information Society, such an analysis is no longer necessary. On the contrary, the managers of an organisation are now far more likely to decide that a documentation unit needs computerising. In tourism, many information managers have faced such a situation, without previously being consulted.

> Computerising a centre is a serious decision. It is costly and takes time to complete.
>
> Computerisation involves all the staff of the Centre, and cannot be done without their full cooperation. The documentation centre must lead the project, both at its inception and during its realisation.

Indeed, information technology and database management of documents provide the personnel of the Centre not just with new tools but they also change radically the methods and working environment of the Centre. This explains why the success of computerisation depends on the full participation of the Centre's staff, and cannot simply be carried out by an outside service provider or solely by information technologists.

The following recommendations constitute a step-by-step process aimed at helping the staff of a documentation centre set up a project and see it through to completion successfully.

4.1 Planning the project

This includes two stages:

- The identification and the positioning of the project,

- A feasibility study which is based on an assessment of the Centre and which describes the project and its priorities.

4.1.1 Identifying the project

This step sets out the objectives of the project (its importance, scope, internal and external use etc.), the changes it will cause in the organisation of the Centre's staff's work, and the overall duration of the project from the feasibility study through to the installation of the selected IT system and its use.

4.1.2 The feasibility study

This is the longest and most important part of the project as it is based on a detailed and complete functional analysis of the operations of the Centre. It should be remembered that computerising a Centre is a costly undertaking, which should not be being carried out in an approximate or arbitrary manner. It must be done with precision and it demands clarity in means and purpose. The computerisation requires a forecast, structure and organisation of the work to be completed. The feasibility study must provide these, and the study is executed in two phases. First, it begins by analysing the existing work and structure of the Centre. Second it sets out a detailed plan for the computerisation of the Centre.

4.1.2.1 An inventory of the Centre's holdings and services

About three months are needed to provide an assessment of the state and functioning of an average-sized centre. If the Centre already produces statistical fact sheets and an annual activity report, then less time may be needed. (These documents are described in detail in Part II of this handbook).

Assessing the Centre requires a detailed and methodical inventory of its functioning. The following steps are recommended:

1. A restatement of the IDRC's role in the Tourism Administration, its history, evolution and major transformations, its budget.

2. A presentation of the staff, the number of employees, their status, qualifications and technical competencies, the hours worked (if part-time), availability for training and the tasks fulfilled by everyone.

3. A description of the Centre's equipment: PCs, typewriters, photocopier(s), telephones, faxes, number of desks, chairs, tables, lighting, stationery, documentary material.

4. Preparation of a plan of the premises. Providing a plan of the surface area and layout of the premises is important for cabling the Centre.

5. Identifying the composition of the document holdings. The volume and typology of the documents available, as well as their annual growth should be given. The following table may be used for this. It is important to calculate the volume growth of the Centre's documents, as this will affect its IT needs, especially, for example, if a tourism photo-library is to be digitised.

THE COMPOSITON OF THE DOCUMENT HOLDINGS AND THEIR DEVELOPMENT

Typology of documents	Volume	Annual increase in %
Articles		
Books		
Brochures and leaflets		
Bulletin of statistics		
Clipping files		
Legislation and legal texts		
List of professional tourism actors and organisations		
Minutes of colloquia		
Official journal of government		
Press conferences and ministerial speeches		
Regional documentary files		
Reports		
Signaletic bibliographies		
Studies		
Thematic documentary files		
University theses		

6. Analysing documentary tools: this involves specifying the use of thesauruses, lexicons, classification tables and shelf-marking systems for different types of documents, for their indexing and classification. Loan files, subject catalogues, author catalogues and classified catalogues must be analysed with their internal organisation indicated. For example, an classified catalogue file should specify the number of racks and types of records (by theme, by region, by country etc.). These catalogues are directly involved in the computerisation process, as each record or information card will ultimately be entered into the computerised documentation database.

7. Presenting documentary products (layout and internal organisation): this should be done so that their computerisation may be carried out. IT makes it possible to automate the creation of catalogues, selective bibliographies, signaletic bibliographies, press reviews or press tables of contents reviews etc.

8. Describing the processing of information: this involves describing how information is processed in the Centre. The following table may be used for aid.

A DESCRIPTION OF THE PROCEDURES FOR PROCESSING DOCUMENTATION

Activity	Review	Article	Book	Staff member
Dates of order and arrival in Centre	10'	10'	10'	Name of the person carrying out the task
Accessioning and preparing document				
Shelf-marking				
Catalogue record (card)				
Analysis of document				
Indexing				
Typing and proof-reading				
Cut and paste				
Ordering and classifying records (or cards)				
Filing away records (or cards)				
Shelving documents				
TOTAL TIME SPENT :				

This description allows the time spent on processing documents to be calculated. It indicates which tasks may be computerised and how much time may be saved. The list of procedures should be carried out for each person processing documents and should be timed.

9. Presenting and describing the services of the IDRC using the following table

A DESCRIPTION OF DOCUMENTATION SERVICES

Staff member(s)	Activities	Time required
	INFORMATION RETRIEVAL	
	One-off retrievalReceiving visitors/readers to the Centre	
	Retrospective retrieval	
	DEVELOPING PRODUCTS	
	Case files	
	CataloguesCompendiums of legislation and laws	
	Current bibliographies	
	Lists of actors	
	Press reviews	
	Selective bibliographies	
	OTHER SERVICES	
	Budget management	
	Document archiving	
	External loans via correspondence and follow-up	
	Internal loans and follow-up	
	Ordering publications	
	Periodical subscriptions	
	Photocopying articles	
	Providing training courses and organising work of interns	
	Replying to mail	
	Replying to telephone requests	
	Reproducing documents	

10. Determining the needs of users and formulating indicators of satisfaction. These functions should be taken into account when selecting IT hardware. It is necessary not only to analyse the number and typology of present and potential users, but also their needs. The second part of this handbook describes the methods for collecting such information.

4.1.2.2 The description of the computerisation project

Once an inventory of the Centre's holdings has been completed, the feasibility study should set out a description of the computerisation project. Two types of situation may arise. First, the computerisation is part of a general shift to computerisation by the Tourist Authority. In this case, the Centre should seek to integrate itself as best as possible within this overall project. Second, the Centre is seeking to computerise itself autonomously.

If computerisation is imposed as part of an overall project, the key issue revolves around the discussions with the information technologists in charge of the project. The choice of software will then clearly depend on the hardware system selected (documentation software is not the same for IBM-compatible PCs or for Apple systems). The advantage of being part of such a general project stems from the fact that the basic IT equipment is usually provided (computers, word-processing software, printers, scanners, Internet connections etc.). In this context, the feasibility study will be short but thorough and will focus exclusively on documentary needs. This involves in selecting the appropriate documentation software as well as software for intelligence gathering and knowledge management etc.

If the computerisation is undertaken autonomously, then it must be promoted within the NTA, and the following steps should be taken into account:

- Is the computerisation project to be undertaken by an external service provider or by the documentation centre itself? The costs of both options should be compared.

- A job specification should be drafted to fix the present priorities of the Centre as well as its future needs.

- A call for tender should be drafted.

- The budget should be calculated.

- The various steps for implementing the project should be set out.

In all cases, the description of the computerisation project should cover the development of the future priorities of the system, which should be included in the job specification. These include:

The priorities for processing information:

To create the data entry forms:

- The obligatory fields should be specified, so that a bibliographic description can only be computerised if these obligatory fields are filled in (date, author, shelf mark etc.);

- The search fields should be determined (author, title, descriptor, date of publication etc.);

- The volume of information to be processed should be indicated, and the existence of previous document records should be specified;

- The annual increase in information should be given;

- The on-line documentary tools should be specified and whether they will be used to index each field (for example the thesaurus and its levels of hierarchy, lexicons, open and closed reference lists);

- The desired controls on each field should be indicated so as to manage errors and confidentiality;

- The number of persons who may enter data interactively at the same time should be fixed. This is important in the choice of software, which should be available on several computers as well as being multi-functional.

- The safeguard system should be defined, as should the frequency for making back-up copies.

The priorities for documentation services:

- The various ways of searching for information need to be taken into account (a simple search in a field with truncation and a Boolean search (a search formulation using logical operators).

- All the products to be created need to be mentioned (bibliographical products, labels, lists, tables etc.);

- It is necessary to specify if loans and orders are to be managed.

4.2 Carrying out the project

4.2.1 Drafting the job specification

The job specification is a document aimed at presenting all the information necessary for sub-contractors to be able to provide a quantitative and costed reply. It is a technical document to which subcontractors may refer, and which is also a contractual document for the call for tender. In other words, it is a document for outside service providers, which sets out concisely the needs of the Centre. It details the functional specificities and the technical architecture of the IT system. The annexes of the job specification cover documents which are to be completed by suppliers and returned. These include:

- a check list for evaluating the proposed software;

- a check list covering the costs involved;

- delivery schedules and a calendar for setting up the system.

The job specification should also insist that suppliers provide a list of other clients/sites equipped with the software offered, as well as the addresses, telephone numbers etc. of other users who may be contacted for a possible visit.

The functional specifications of the system

The priorities which are defined in the description of the project may be used to draw up a list of functions required of the future information system. The following is a proposed list:

a) Generalities
   Integration of the entire documentary holding
   Capacity for volume evolution
   Ergonomics of the product
   Help to users
   Error management

b) Management of holdings
   Database updating
   Managing user profiles and confidentiality
   File entry and modification
   Indexing entries, using thesauruses, lexicons, open and closed lists
   Multi-criteria and multi-field searches using Boolean operators and logical operators

Print and export formats/automatic publishing of lists, catalogues, labels, screen displays, printing on paper, diskette exports etc.
Database export/import (with different files and formats)

c) Extended functions
   Loan management
   Automatic recall notice
   Order management
   Periodicals management
      Accessioning and circulation of periodicals
      subscriptions
   Statistics of
      consultations
      loans
      indexing with descriptors

d) Product openness
   Interface with other software/programmes
   Other functions/modules

e) Word and text processing

The technical IT architecture

This indicates the power of the database server and the number of workstations it must serve, the number of workstations directly connected, the number of printers, scanners and the number of programmes connected to the system. The supplier should be asked to provide a full description of this architecture and indicate the capacity of the material to evolve.

Delivery and installation delays

The supplier should provide a schedule for installing the hard- and software. The schedule should include: the delivery and setting up of equipment, the configuration of software and operating systems, as well as training the Centre's staff.

A cost check list

SUPPLIES Quantity and type	Unit cost excl. VAT, before discount	Discount	Unit cost excl. VAT, after discount	Unit cost inc. VAT, after discount	Total cost
HARDWARE					
server					
personal computer					
printer					
scanner					
setting up equipment					
SOFTWARE					
documentation programmes					
order and loan programmes					
economic intelligence programmes					
word processing					
other necessary software					
OPTIONS					
specific IT products if necessary					
cabling if necessary					
TRAINING					
on-site training per day					
off-site training per day					
ASSISTANCE					
days per person					
PROJECT EXECUTION					
days per person					
ANNUAL MAINTENANCE					
hardware					
software					
on-site maintenance					

4.2.2 The call of tender and the choice of the IT system

The call for tender is an official document which consists of sending a job specification to suppliers, accompanied by a letter setting out the objective and modalities of the computerisation. Assessing the results of the tender involves examining the quality and cost of different systems and software, which may be tested on other sites. It is also useful to contact user clubs when possible and other users suggested by prospective contractors.

4.3 Recommendations

4.3.1 Choosing documentation software[13]

Documentation software is made up of a set of programmes which allow databases to be created, updated, interrogated and information to be published. Using such software is a prime necessity for a Centre that needs to be computerised. Many different types of programmes exist, at very different costs. To select software, selection criteria should be set out in advance, and defined in the job specification. It is recommended to use a checklist for assessing programmes and to consult comparative studies made of programmes which are printed in the trade press or by specialised companies. Apart from the criteria presented above, the "priorities for the computerisation project" and "the functional specifications of the system" set out in the job specification, this handbook's recommendations are based on choosing programmes for multi-terminal systems capable of handling several databases. The programme should also be able to manage a multi-lingual thesaurus, or at least manage the descriptors with linguistic equivalence, as well as the capacity for electronic document management. Without going into technical detail here, it should be mentioned that programmes for managing documents electronically are able to carry out all the classical functions of a documentation programme, but are also able to digitise documents. In other words, they can store full text, though this requires a scanner and possibly a CDROM engraver to stock and archive documents.

Apart from allowing a truly, on-line tourism library to be set up, or images/photos and press reviews to be managed, a electronic document management programme is a powerful tool which allows the accumulation of full text information about national tourism policy and makes it more widely available. Such information includes: grey literature, studies and reports by the National Tourism Administration, texts relating to the national tourism regulation, press conferences and ministerial speeches. All of these documents relate to the work of the Tourism Administration, as to its organisation chart, mission reports, know-how etc. Such documents may be linked to bibliographic description.

Electronic document management was deliberately excluded from the functions of the job specification checklist because such programmes are more expensive than traditional documentation management programmes.

4.3.2 Personnel training

Training should be carried out both on-site and on the premises of the software provider, depending on the number of people involved and the specificity of the training.

---

[13] The United Nations Educational, Scientific and Cultural Organization (UNESCO) develops, maintains and distributes free-of-charge the CDS/ISIS software, an information storage and retrieval system for the computerized management of structured non-numerical databases, particularly bibliographic references. (http://www.unesco.org/webworld/isis/isis.htm)

Training should cover documentation management programmes, librarianship, ordering of documents/books etc. It is strongly recommended that such training takes place in two phases. The first phase should take place on site, and should accompany the setting up of the hardware and software. It should be based on the direct example of the documentation centre, and should by used to establish the architecture of the database, the products to be printed and extracted from the database. Forms for data entry and retrieval should be prepared prior to this training period, so that the period may be used to create them directly. A second, complementary, more-detailed training period should focus on the databases the Centre has created, and should so be used to examine and resolve any problems experienced by the users of the databases.

4.3.3 Product assistance and maintenance

This should by carried out by telephone and by an on-site visit if necessary. The supplier should stipulate annual maintenance conditions: on-site visits, the supply of new software versions, user clubs, costs involved in a contractual document etc.

4.3.4 The creation of the databases

Before the programmes and databases are set up, it is strongly recommended to design models of data entry forms (i.e. computer screen entry forms), based on coding sheets, though the latter may be scrapped once data is entered directly into the database. Such sheets should be created by the information managers, several months before the creation of the databases. Each field, within each sheet, should be discussed at length and tested, in view of its uses. The following pages provide some examples of such data entry forms and/or coding sheets, which may be used as models for creating databases in the Information and Documentation Resource Centre of the National Tourism Administration.

(The fields in bold are search fields, in other words fields on which it is possible to conduct searches and retrieve information.)

Database of bibliographical references

Type of document	**Shelf-mark**	**ISBN/ISSN/ISRN**
Title		
Title of periodical	**Issue No**	
Volume	Pages	**Language**
Sponsoring organisation	**Author**	**Corporate author**
Publisher	Place	**Date**
Summary		
Subject Descriptor		**Geographical descriptor**
Publication accessibility		
Person responsible for date entry		Date of entry

Database of tourism professionals

Organisation		Acronym	
Parent organisation		**Address**	
Post code	Town	Country	
Telephone	Fax	Email	Internet site
Title	**Name**	**Function**	
Legal structure		**Staff**	Turnover
Subject descriptor / sector of activity			
Geographic descriptor / geographic zone of activity			
Fields of research (if research institute)			
Events/ Partnerships			
Information dissemination networks		Notes	
Person responsible for data entry		Date of entry	

Database of tourism laws and regulations

Type of text	No of text	Date of text	
Date of publication in Official Journal		Page	
Subject or title	Shelf-mark		Publisher
Subject descriptor		**Geographical descriptor**	
Person responsible for data entry		**Date of entry**	

Further information about the preceding fields is given in Chapter 4 of Part II of this handbook.

4.3.5 Implementing computerisation standards

A key factor in successfully computerising document holdings concerns the formulation, application and respect of common standards of data entry and indexing when the data entry forms are prepared. These standards should be discussed and adopted by everyone likely to be involved in data entry for the databases, and should be set out in a notebook or file. As for keyword indexing, if this is done using a thesaurus or pre-established list of keywords, then the only problems likely to occur relate to the choice of up-case or lower-case letters.

The question of standards is particularly important for open data entry fields, such as the author field. For this, the following standard may be adopted :

    Name: in capitals   First name : small letters   separator : a comma
    Example: DUPOND, George

Another example could relate to the name of an organisation and its acronym, as well as its preference language: WORLD TOURISM ORGANIZATION (WTO) / ORGANISATION MONDIALE DU TOURISME (OMT)

The problems of data entry are greatly reduced if each field is assigned a reference list (where possible) in the form of a lexicon for fields such as "type of document", "legal status", "periodical" etc. It is also recommended to use as many ISO (or national) standards as possible in cataloguing documents. These norms should also be used, where possible, in producing documentary publications: bibliographies, labels, lists, tables, catalogues, press reviews etc.

II METHODOLOGICAL AND TECHNICAL GUIDE

II.1 IDENTIFYING DEMAND

It is impossible to make an assessment or begin any project for organising or creating an IDRC without first identifying the demand for information that needs to be met, which is the very objective of the IDRC. The whole organisation of the Centre is geared to meeting and processing the demand for information in the most effective and efficient manner. Dealing with the demand for information is simply the *raison d'être* of the Centre. This constitutes the principal difference between a documentation centre and a library. Libraries have a more general vocation, whereas documentation centres are necessarily specialised, focusing on meeting a specific, sectoral demand for information. It is inconceivable to set up a documentation centre without there being a clear demand by users, while libraries may strive more to promote culture and make it accessible. From this point of view, the main function of a library is to "conserve knowledge". For a documentation centre, it is to "disseminate information" via documentary products and services[14]. For these reasons, it is vital to identify and understand the forms of demand the Centre will deal with, prior to its creation, modification or computerisation. Two forms of survey can be used to do this: direct surveys and indirect surveys.

1.1 A direct survey

Such a survey is carried out :

- using individual interviews with experts, selected in advance; by organising round-table discussions which bring together potential users and various categories of actors;

- through the use of questionnaires with closed questions (which are answered by ticking a "yes" or "no" box) and with open questions (allowing respondents to make their own observations).

Individual interviews, with a selection of people in charge of, or specialised in certain areas of tourism, should make it possible not only to identify their needs for information, but also establish their profiles by identifying fields of knowledge, areas of competencies, experience and missions which they have to carry out in area of activity and which could be of interest to other actors. Such information makes it possible to practice a selective dissemination of information (SDI), catering to the individual needs of each actor. It also makes it possible to create a directory of experts which may be used in developing a "who knows what" chart within the NTA. This in turn will permit the creation of a flow chart of knowledge and know-how that can ultimately be completed with knowledge management techniques. Individual interviews can provide detailed information, and may be perfected over time, as the survey is conducted. If many people are involved, the process becomes ite laborious, in which case questionnaires should be used.

---

14 It is of course entirely feasible that the IDRC of the National Tourist Administration also houses a specialised library on tourism, in which case it will fulfil both the functions of conserving knowledge and disseminating information.

Round-table discussions bring together particular categories of actors (who may prefer to be informed by electronic means, or who may prefer receiving paper documents etc.) or actors in certain sectors (those working in legislation and law, those producing statistics etc.). Round-tables make it possible to provide greater detail of their needs for tourism information.

Questionnaires may be distributed to all personnel of the National Tourism Administration in order to identify their needs. But this method alone tends to be insufficient, as only about 50 percent of all questionnaires sent out are returned, at most.

Mixed-surveys associate the distribution of questionnaires and round-table discussions, which are sometimes further completed by individual interviews.

1.2 Indirect surveys

Indirect surveys draw on data collected throughout the year from the visitor statistics of the IDRC, loans of documents, photocopied articles, bibliographical demands and other information searches conducted. They include discussions with users, a knowledge of current affairs in the sector, an overview of the general and trade press, all of which make it possible to anticipate the demand for information. General knowledge of the economic and social developments that may affect tourism makes it possible to compile documentary files in advance: for example, in the wake of an ecological disaster (such as the sinking of a petrol tanker) beaches may be polluted or government policies affected, such as a change to the rate of Value Added Tax (VAT) or equivalent tax.

1.3 The typology of information users

There are two types of users of the IDRC of a National Tourism Administration: internal users and external users.

1.3.1 Internal users

Internal users are varied. The NTA will include personnel with purely administrative functions, such as human resources, personnel training, IT services etc. It will also have staff responsible for studying and formulating tourism policy, relating to laws and regulations, taxation, regional development, sustainable development, tourist markets (business tourism, cultural tourism, health tourism, leisure markets), tourism infrastructures (hotels, campsites, transport etc.) and statistics related to both national and international tourism.

1.3.2 External users

Generally speaking, the demand for information which is made to the Tourism Administration's IDRC is professional in nature and does not come from the general public. That said, some IDRCs may be responsible for replying to requests for travel information, concerning the organisation of holidays, the weather, geography, transport, prices etc. If the Centre does not treat such requests for information, it should nevertheless be able to orient them to organisations capable of replying.

Leaving aside tourists and the general public, the profiles of persons outside the NTA who may ask for information from the Centre include:

- students preparing a degree/diploma in tourism (master's dissertation, thesis);

- teachers preparing courses;

- researchers seeking to study documents which are at the leading edge of research, such as specialised journals or reports etc.;

- persons seeking to set up private companies and searching for information about legislation as well as technical information for creating firms;

- service providers (consulting companies, market research organisations etc.) which are carrying out studies for clients;

- investors seeking more information about a market they wish to invest in;

- architects, urban planners and development planners concerned with development planning (projects and regional development) in tourism;

- tour operators and other tourist promoters seeking promotional documentation, press conferences, conference proceedings, marketing plans etc.;

- elected politicians and policy-makers, who may be responsible for drafting official reports relating to tourism;

- government employees from other administrations linked to tourism (public works, industry, agriculture, culture, environment and health), who are working on tourism-related issues;

- journalists seeking for precise statistical information, case files, special reports, clipping files, photographs, slides etc.

> For all these persons, the request for information is expressed in a similar manner:
>
> they seek to obtain as rapidly and as easily as possible the most detailed, most relevant and least costly information relating to their subject of inquiry.

1.4 A permanent procedure for controlling and assessing users' satisfaction[15]

Analysing users' demands is even more important and pertinent in the age of Internet. As has already been shown, the documentation function has been thoroughly transformed by Internet and the New Economy. Internet allows everyone to access and edit information without needing to manage it nor enrich it. Internauts have a worldwide library at their disposal as well as powerful search engines to guide them. This raises the question of what the value added of information provided by an IDRC is. How can such availability of documentation be enriched? How should the IDRC position its information supply in relation to the multitude of portals available, from press services to governmental sites? What should it offer users and in what order of priority?

To answer all these questions, it is necessary to set up a procedure for permanently surveying and identifying users' present and future needs. All types of request for information which reach the IDRC should be identified and classified: requests by phone, by email, by letter, fax, requests for loans, visitors to the Centre. Each request for information should be recorded on a form or slip. Analysis of these forms then makes it possible not only to define users' profiles and the typology of demand, but also to draft the IDRC's annual activity report, which assesses the overall demand for information addressed to the Centre and examines the extent to which the Centre' supply matches this demand. Filling out such forms may indeed be laborious on a daily basis, but it is an essential procedure in assessing permanently the quantity and quality of users' demands, in order to ensure that the Centre's output evolves.

The forms presented below should be adapted to the needs and choices made by the IDRC, depending on the conditions of access to its holdings.

Access is determined by the persons in charge of the Centre, according to the communication and information policy of the National Tourism Administration and the means made available to the Centre.

---

[15] ISO 11620 is relative to assessment indicators for libraries.

1.4.1 INTERNAL REQUEST FORM

(To be completed by the user or the information manager.)

User's name

Department

Date of request

Nature of the request

Services		Requests needing a product to be created	
Book orders and subscriptions	❏	Bibliographical search by subject, retrospective etc.	❏
Consultation of a book or periodical	❏	Search for legislation and regulation	❏
Book loans and returns	❏	Search for tourism actors and experts	❏
Reprography of an article	❏	Search for statistics	❏
Reproducing a document (number of pages)	❏	Case files or press review	❏
Digitising a document (number of pages)	❏	Dossier on regulations	❏

Other ❏

URGENT

If the request is urgent, please tick the box ❏

1.4.2 EXTERNAL REQUEST FORM

Requests for information arriving at the IDRC by telephone, fax, email, or letter.
(The form is to be completed by the person answering the request.)

Name: person or organisation
Legal status (student, consultant, travel agent etc.)
Date of request

Subject of the request:
(free text or specific question asked)

Request dealt with by: Name:	Date:

Request needing documents to be sent	Yes:	No:

(specify type of document sent)

Time taken to meet request:

1.4.3 VISITOR REQUEST FORM
(To be completed by visitor.)

Previous user of the IDRC yes/no   Date:

Name of person and/or organisation

Address

Telephone/email

Objective of research:

Area of research:

Documents consulted (shelf-marks or names of reviews/journals):

Information obtained: do the information and services of the documentation Centre answer to your information request(s)?

❏ Completely   ❏ Partially   ❏ Not at all

Would you like to receive FREE information about the activities of the Centre and to receive its publications (name of newsletter or products)?

II.2 CONSTITUTING THE DOCUMENT HOLDINGS

Once the profile of the Centre's users is known and the type or requests for information have been identified and analysed, the Centre's holdings should be constituted and classified to meet these needs.

2.1 What is a document?

Documentary information comprises scientific and technical information. Whenever the notion of a document is referred to as an object (or support) bearing knowledge or information, it is referred to here as Scientific or Technical Information (STI): i.e. data or information which meets the needs of a specialised public, as opposed to journalistic information, relating to events or aimed at the general public.

For a document to be considered as STI it must meet the following criteria:

- authenticity: the author of the document must be identified;

- reliability: the document must be verifiable. Documents that can be falsified (especially when recorded electronically) are not considered as legal proof;

- accessibility: it must be possible to locate a document and consult it, using normal means of reproduction and dissemination;

- relevancy: documents held by the Centre should be relevant and up to date, in order to satisfy users' demands.

Several categories and several types of documents exist. Three categories may be identified according to their state of elaboration:

Primary documents: these are original documents in the sense that they contain original information. They include: biographies, patents, communiqués, monographs, books, standards, reports, brochures etc.;

Secondary documents or derived documents: they are aimed at orienting the user. They point out or analyse primary documents. These are the working tools for information managers, and include: abstracts or summaries, bibliographies, indexes, catalogues, case files, directories, press reviews etc.;

Tertiary documents: are documents which present either a summary of primary documents or an anthology of analysis of secondary documents such as bibliographies of bibliographies.

2.2 The typology of documents

The following typology is provided as an indication. Further information is given by the work of the ISO, especially the standard 5127 which relates to documentation vocabulary.

Non-periodical documents distinguished by their form: acts, proceedings, atlases, brochures, maps, books, manuscripts, plans, tables, leaflets etc.

Non-periodical documents distinguished by their content: abridged versions, anthologies, autobiographies, cartoons, biographies, dictionaries, case files, encyclopaedias, glossaries, guides, indexes, lexicons, handbooks, manuals, monographs, organisation charts, music scores, minutes, reports, collections of texts, scenarios, thesauruses, theses, treaties, transcriptions, transpositions etc.

Serials: these are fascicles or volumes which run in series, in chronological or numerical order. They include reviews, journals, directories, series, periodicals, monographs etc.

Images and audiovisual documents: these cover both cinematographic recordings as well as sound recordings (audiocassettes, sound cassettes, compact disks), video recordings (optical disks, videocassettes, videodisks) and fixed images (posters, albums, cards, slides, microfiches, photos, pictograms, transparencies etc.). All such documents require special equipment to be viewed or listened to.

Electronic documents: CDROMs, digitised optical disks, programmes, diskettes, DVDs and other digitised documents with images or texts etc.

2.3 The specificity of tourism holdings

The tourism sector generates extremely wide and rich document holdings in terms of contents and supports. It is therefore possible to distinguish several sets of tourism documents which the IDRC of a Tourism Administration may have to manage:

Books or monographs: these include published books, which are available in libraries and present a detailed and complete study of a field in the economy of tourism, the sociology of leisure, the development of regions, the geography of tourism and the legislation on tourism. These documents are mainly made up of publications by researchers, school manuals, and works of a methodological and economic nature, published by institutional organisations.

Grey literature: this set of documents is by far the most important in the tourism holdings. "Grey" or "underground" literature refers to the immaterial stock of knowledge, in other words, documents which are not published within commercial distribution networks. This wealth of information includes, in particular, research studies and reports, methodological and procedural documents, directives and various other memoranda. The National Tourist Authority is the main generator of such literature, in as much as it is responsible for the national policy on tourism, development policies, regulating the various activities of the sector, carrying out surveys needed to compile statistics on tourism, especially the satellite accounts of the sector. These documents are much in demand as they are up to date and provide relevant information. A standardised international report number exists (ISRN[16]) which helps access to this wealth of information, as well as its preservation and full use.

Periodicals, the tourism trade press: journals, reviews and tourism magazines are indispensable tools for drawing up press reviews, clipping files and current affairs dossiers, or for finding references to new publications. All countries have access to a national and international tourism press, but many also have a regional tourism press. The tourism trade press may be organised by theme or subject (hotels, catering, travel etc.) or it may be general. It may be aimed at professionals (dealing with different activities in the sector) or it may follow on from research. Much of this press is now available on Internet.

Reference works on tourism: this category of research tools are more or less specialised and are frequently used. Reference works in tourism include dictionaries and encyclopaedias on tourism, tools of tourism linguistics (thesauruses, glossaries, lexicons), thematic directories (on hotels, camping, tourism offices etc.), directories of tourism professionals (travel agents, transport companies, researchers etc.), calendars of tourism events (holidays, seminars, public holidays, festivals etc.), geographical atlases and atlases specialised in the spatial organisation of tourism (atlases of coastlines, mountains, touristic cities) and professional manuals (how to open a hotel, a restaurant, a travel agency etc.).

Tourism records: a distinction may be made between archives which have reached a state of permanent conservation and "records"[17] that are still living documents which may be consulted by users, especially within the Tourism Administration. This group of documents relates to the history and organisation of the NTA: founding texts, programmes and budgets, successive ministerial press conferences, minutes of assemblies, seminar proceedings, studies and publications, international and multilateral accords, partnership conventions, legislation and regulations etc.

---

16 International standard technical report number, ISO 10444, 1994.
17 The English term "records" refers to documents considered in their dimension of proof or usefulness to the perfomance of the activities of the issuing entity, as opposed to "documents", which only takes into account their normartive content. Since it has no strict equivalent in French, "records" is translated as "documents d'archives".

Documents promoting tourism: these include tourism brochures, leaflets and posters. They exist to promote or generate publicity for a particular type of tourism activity or region.

Tourism guides and maps: Geographical guides and tourism maps are available for nearly all towns, countries and regions of the world. Guides may also cover certain themes, such as gastronomy, hotels, restaurants, bed & breakfast accommodation etc.

Tourism films and photos: this group of documents may by itself constitute a photo-library or film-library.

All these various groups of documents are produced by tourism professionals as well as by institutional and public actors in the tourism sector. A National Tourism Administration's IDRC should acquire, classify and make use of all these types of documents.

2.4 The acquisition of documents

To build up the documentary holdings in tourism, information and documents within the major sets of tourism documentation must be assembled, so as to best meet the demands and profiles of the Centre's users. For example, documentation centres which supply tourists and travellers with information should acquire guides and maps, promotional documents, a photo-library, leaflets, brochures and posters. An IDRC for the staff of the NTA, professional organisations and researchers should gather documentation which is more economic and statistic in its nature, made up of monographs, articles, records and above all grey literature.

To gather such information correctly it is important to identify and know the main sources producing information.

2.4.1 Internal sources

The usefulness of holding interviews with the staff of the NTA (employees and experts) has already been stressed. Such interviews allow not just the information needs of future users to be identified, but also provide knowledge of the documents produced within the various departments of the NTA and so help them to be acquired. It should be stressed, however, that IDRCs often run up division of work between departments and the withholding of information, especially within government organisations. To tackle such difficulties, it may be useful to formalise relations between the Centre and the other departments of the Tourism Administration through a "Documentation Charter" (see the model provided at the end of this chapter). Such a Charter sets out the conditions for acquiring documents and requires departments to deposit a copy of all documents produced by the Administration with the Centre. It is also possible to obtain an administrative circular requiring the legal deposit of documents with the IDRC.

> **ADMINISTRATIVE DIRECTIVE FOR THE DEPOSIT OF DOCUMENTS**
>
> (addressed by the Director of the Tourism Administration to all heads of departments and units under his/her authority)
>
> Two copies of all documents (studies, reports, economic and research memoranda) and publications produced or sponsored by this administration must be deposited with the Information and Documentation Resource Centre, within two weeks (at most) of their publication or acquisition.
>
> It is generally recommended to provide the IDRC will all publications received from outside the Tourist Authority so that they may be available to all.
>
> Only under these conditions, together with your full application of this directive will it be possible for this administration to constitute archives and document holdings that can meet everyone's needs.

2.4.2 External sources

The Centre may turn to the following sources to find out which documents it should acquire:

- catalogues of publishers or bookshops, in paper format or on Internet. These catalogues present documents which may be bought;

- general library catalogues and directories of international periodical publications (http://www.issn.org);

- annual lists of publications distributed by tourism organisations and associations nationally, internationally or regionally, as well as by governmental organisations, research institutes and universities which deal with tourism;

- analytical bibliographies and accession lists published by libraries and documentation centres of professional or institutional organisations which directly deal with the tourism sector;

- book indexes;

- directories and yearbooks providing addresses and practical information about tourism actors, tourism resources, cultural heritage, and touristic activities etc.;

- the general and specialised trade press which presents analyses of publications.

2.5 The Centre's acquisition policy

Once sources have been identified, it is important to formulate an acquisition policy. It is made up of two parts. The first part sets out the selection criteria of documents, relating to their reliability, their current relevance, the recognition of their authors and publishers: in short criteria which allow the relevance of the document to be judged. The second part analyses choices to be made, subject to the function and nature of the Centre's activities, its users, its degree of specialisation, its editorial policy, and the existence of other information and documentation resource centres.

2.5.1 Acquiring documents

Documents may be acquired by:

buying publications, which necessitates filling out an order form. Such a form may be used for one or several documents grouped together. It is usually made up of a table with several columns, headed: "quantity", "author", "title", "place of publication", "publisher", "date of publication", and "price". The forms should include the name and full address of the Centre, the date of the order and its number. It is recommended that a book/documentation order is accompanied by a letter, which includes the following:

> Dear Sir or Madam,
>
> Please find enclosed a list of documents and/or subscriptions of journals which we would like to receive as soon as possible.
>
> .... copies of the (pro-forma/final) invoice should be sent to us, and should take account of our right to a ... (tax deduction/rebate etc.).
>
> We look forward to receiving these document(s) as soon as possible.
>
> Yours faithfully,
>
> Head of Documentation Centre

by subscribing to a publication of which the Centre has asked to receive a specimen copy. The following letter may be sent to the subscription manager asking for such a copy:

> Dear Sir or Madam,
>
> To expand its documentary holdings, the Information and Documentation Resource Centre of the National Tourism Administration would be grateful if you could send us a specimen copy of (name of title) along with the conditions for subscribing to this journal/press service.
>
> We look forward to receiving the copy and this information as soon as possible.
>
> Yours faithfully,
>
> Head of Documentation Centre

by receiving donations: numerous international or research organisations distribute their documents free of charge;

by exchanging documentation: documents are often exchanged between institutional tourism organisations. A convention for exchanging documents may be adopted with interested parties in order to make the exchange procedure official and systematic.

2.6 The Documentation Charter / The Quality Charter

This is an innovative management tool. It is a way of transcribing and establishing clearly the documentation policy of the IDRC, its objectives, instruments and rules. The Charter should be discussed and then validated by the top management of the Tourism Administration for it to be accepted by users. It should be brief in dealing with each subject and capable of modification depending on changing circumstances (and should not exceed two pages). The Charter will include several headings, each made up of a number of "articles".

The Quality Charter

Introduction: should set out the objective of the Charter as well as the rules governing its management and operation.

The role and mission of the documentation centre: the goal of the Centre should be restated (to identify, collect and disseminate information within the Tourism Administration, in order to manage and retrieve the information produced in the Administration's departments rapidly).

The reception and dissemination of information: should set out the rules for the departments and personnel of the NTA, for example:

Article 1: In order to identify and record information, all mail arriving in the postal service of the NTA should be passed on to the Information and Documentation Resource Centre which will be responsible for distributing it.

Article 2: Staff of the NTA receiving documents which may be of interest in updating the documentary database should inform the Centre and pass the document, or a copy of its table of contents, to the Centre for registration.

Article 3: as the IDRC is responsible for holding a running inventory of legal texts relating to tourism, it should receive copies of all official texts (decrees, circulars etc.) produced by the NTA's departments.

Research reports and grey literature: the Centre requests that two copies of every study or research report produced or financed by the NTA's departments are deposited with it. As the IDRC is the living memory of the Authority, it is responsible for conserving all documents produced by the Tourism Administration's departments. For this reason it is a depositary of acts, proceedings, conventions, conferences and clipping files, ministerial speeches and presentations, publicity campaigns, touristic brochures, technical guides and other so-called grey literature documents.

Orders and purchases of documents: the ways in which the IDRC acquires documents (if forms need to be filled in etc.) should be set out. It should be borne in mind that the centralised management of purchases helps avoid buying documents twice.

Periodicals: it should be specified whether or not the Centre is responsible for managing all subscriptions, with its own budget and how publications are ordered.

Should the IDRC wish to create a Quality Charter, it should include the above information and state all the services the Centre provides its users, as well as the time taken to carry out these services.

II.3 CLASSIFYING AND MAKING AN INVENTORY OF THE DOCUMENT HOLDING

Several sets of documents were identified previously relating to tourism. Before classifying these, three operations need to be carried out:

- accessioning,
- shelf-marking,
- document preparation.

3.1 Accessioning

This makes it possible to keep an inventory of the holdings and to know at all times the number of documents available within each set of documents. It also allows an "accession list" to be drawn up periodically, by the Centre to inform its users.

Books, monographs, reference works, reports, studies and archives are registered in an inventory book or file.

The minimal data for accession includes: the title of the document, the author, the date of publication, and the inventory number. Accession may be completed by noting the way in which documents are acquired, so as to provide information that ultimately may be used to establish a typology of the Centre's documents, according to their mode of acquisition. For archives, a single identifying code should be used so that they can be distinguished from the rest of the holdings, as these are documents produced in-house and will receive special "records management" treatment.

Periodicals: their registration involves daily entry. To do this so-called "Kardex" files may be bought commercially. The specialty of these files is that they are visible. Each periodical has two files: one bears the references of the periodical and the publisher, the other indicates the number (volume and series), as well as the date of publication and reception of the document by the Centre. Accessioning periodicals allows subscriptions to be managed and a permanent inventory of the series to be made.

3.2 Shelf-marking documents

This operation involves indicating where documents are classed and located. Care should be taken in deciding what shelf-mark is to be attributed to a document, as several shelf-mark and classification systems exist. A document's shelf-mark should take into account the ways in which documents are accessed, according to the policy framework of the Centre. It depends on whether the document is on open access or only available via an information manager.

Numerical shelf-marks may be used when documents are on open access. In this case, documents are numbered chronologically and classified by order of arrival or inventory.

Information and Documentation Resource Centres for Tourism
© 2004 World Tourism Organization - ISBN: 92-844-0717-6

It is then easy to return them to their shelf position after consultation. Alphabetical classifications may also be used, for example, according to the author's name. This is especially appropriate for libraries, of a more literary nature.

3.2.1 Shelf-marking tourism holdings

Neither of these two systems really meets the specific needs of tourism holdings. Indeed, numerical classification systems do not reflect fully the multidisciplinary nature of tourism documentation as well as its geographical diversity. On the other hand, alphabetical classifications are not easily applicable to authors of tourism publications. Apart from individual researchers whose works are published and available in bookshops, and who are known in educational and research circles, tourism publications are often produced by corporate authors, in other words organisations, institutions, working groups etc.

> It is suggested that the classification of holdings by an IDRC of a NTA should be alphanumerical or systematic. This involves shelf-marking and ordering documents by field or sector of activity or keyword. Within each field or keyword a number is then attributed chronologically to each document.

To be sure, many classification systems exist. In France, the Universal Decimal Classification and the Dewey Decimal Classification are used most. In English-speaking countries, the Library of Congress Classification is used especially in North America, while the Bliss classification is much used in Great Britain.

These systems classify all human knowledge by category or by discipline. Given their general nature, they are not easily applicable to tourism, which is a new and evolving field characterised by diversity and the fact that it draws on several disciplines in social sciences, including geography, history, economics, sociology, psychology etc.

The following paragraphs provide an example of the type of shelf-marking which could be used in a Tourism Administration.

Books, monographs, reports and studies, in other words all documents that may be stored in shelves will bear alphanumerical shelf-marks according to the specific tourism sector of keyword in question, the choice of keywords being adapted to the overall holdings. This involves drawing up list of keywords and labelling them with a simple or compound noun, for example: "accommodation", "health tourism" etc. Next, the first (three or four) letters of the sector are used in the shelf-mark, e.g.: ACCOM. for "accommodation", "HEA.TOU" for "health tourism". Once this list has been established, documents are then classified numerically, in chronological order of their acquisition, e.g.: ACCOM.21 is the twenty-first document shelved which deals with accommodation.

Similarly, the following sectors may be used to classify documents:

FIELD	Shelf-mark	FIELD	Shelf-mark
Accommodation	ACCOM	Sport	SPO
Business tourism	BUS.TOU	Sustainable tourism	SUST.TOU
Camping	CAM	Technology (information, reservation, e-tourism)	TECH
Catering	CAT	Tourism (general works on tourism)	TOU
Coastlines	COAST	Tourism budget	TOU.BUD
Cultural tourism	CUL.TOU	Tourism economy	TOU.ECO
Forecasting studies	FORE	Tourism events	TOU.EVE
History of tourism	TOU.HIST	Tourism financing	TOU.FIN
Holidays	HOL	Tourism heritage	TOU.HER
Hotels	HOT	Tourism international market	TOU.INT
International arrivals	INT.ARR	Tourism legislation	TOU.LEG
Leisure	LEIS	Tourism management	TOU.MAN
Methodological studies	METH	Tourism national market	TOU.NAT
Motivation studies	MOT	Tourism organisation	TOU.ORG
Mountains	MOUNT	Tourism policy	TOU.POL
National or regional tourism development	TOU.DEV	Tourism promotion	TOU.PROM
National tourism accounts	TOU.ACC	Tourism vocational training	TOU.TRA
Nature conservation	NAT.CON	Transport	TRAN
Parks and natural reserves	PARK	Travel organisers	TRAV.AGE
Rural areas	RUR	Water tourism	WAT.TOU
Senior citizens tourism	SEN.TOU	Youth tourism	YOU.TOU
Sociology (of leisure or tourism)	SOC		

The above shelf-mark classification is a translation of the system used by the IDRC of the French Tourism Administration. The choice of subject fields or keywords corresponds to the number and importance of documents existing for each field. The system is simple and easy to adapt. New subject fields or keywords may be established, such as "sustainable tourism" or "new technologies", which have generated several publications in recent years. It is also very easy to see how many works are available in each field. In addition, the system is somewhat independent of information technology, as documents relating to a particular field are easily accessible in the shelving. It is not always necessary to locate a document using the computer system or the database of references. This is especially useful in the case of computer failure or when time is not available to make a detailed search. Some documents, such as documents about budgets etc., should be available instantly, without necessitating the use of intermediate tools. This is even easier when such documents are numbered chronologically according to their date of publication and not their entry into the Centre's inventory, e.g.: TOU.BUD.2003 used for all the documents relating to the national tourism budget for 2003.

Geographical documents are classified in the same way, using the first three or four letters of the region, country or continent.

The documents are then stored on the shelves according to the alphabetical order of the shelf-marks. Geographical documents about countries or regions are separated from subject documents. When a geographical document focuses on a particular subject (e.g.: hotels in Japan), then it is classed according to the country.

For the classification of articles, these may be stored in archive boxes on shelves. They may carry a special number to distinguish them from the rest of the documents on the shelves. For example, "0" can be reserved to designate articles relating to each field or for each keyword. Articles on travel organisers and travel activities could start with the shelf mark TRAV.ORG.0. The archive box will be placed at the beginning of all documents of the field. Alternatively, articles could be classified by field and year of publication: e.g. TRAV.ORG.2003 could be used to designate all articles relating to travel agencies in 2003. These archive boxes constitute the clipping files in each subject field of tourism. It is advisable to classify the articles contained in each box by facets or sub-classes. For example, a clipping file on travel activities could include the following sub-classes: travel agencies, tour operators, turnover, employment, labour costs etc.

Periodicals are stored in shelving or filing cabinets designed for them and are classified according to the alphabetical order of their titles.

Reference works are, by definition, consulted a lot. They should be easy to find and access, and so should be stored not in shelves, but in a display unit. Their shelf-mark may be prefixed by "RW_" for reference work.

Publicity and promotional documents may use the same alphanumerical shelf-marking system, as well as having a special storage space, such as in cabinets of hanging files For example, brochures produced by the Tourism Administration could be shelf-marked according to their support (BRO for brochures) and classified according to they year of publication (e.g.: BRO.2003 for all brochures published in 2003). For hanging files, the titles of the brochures should be stated, and they should be classed in alphabetical order by year. If a brochure is updated every year, then the opposite should be done, in other words in alphabetical order of the titles, with each title then being ordered chronologically.

Tourist guides and maps should also have their own storage space and should be classified in alphabetical order, by country or by region and by town.

Tourism archives require their own classification system. It may follow the logic of the shelf-marks used in the Centre, based on activities. These activities, however, do not relate to all types of activities in the tourism sector, but to the activities of the Tourism Administration itself, as it is mainly the documents produced by the NTA and its departments which are archived. Only a classification system which is linked to the functions of the Authority is logically coherent for records management.

3.2.2 A classification table for activities

The preliminary analysis for creating a classification table should identify all the activities linked to the missions and objectives of the NTA, including:

a) the goals and strategies of the organisation,

b) the functions of the organisation on which the pursuit of these goals and objectives is founded,

c) the activities of the organisation which draws together these functions,

d) the work process set up for these activities and specific work,

e) all the various stages which make up these activities,

f) all the concrete actions linked to the stages making up the activities,

g) all recurrent actions linked to each activity, and

h) all documents which exist within the organisation.

The conclusions of the analysis may be set out as a hierarchy of the activities of the Tourist Authority, completed if necessary[18].

It is up to the IDRC to decide how detailed the classification table ought to be, depending on the functions of the NTA. An example of a classification table based on the different functions of the Tourist Administration would be:

---

18 ISO/TR 15489-2, March 2002, page 9.

1 Organisation of tourism	1.1 National organisation	
	1.2 Regional organisation	
2 Tourism budget		
3 Tourism regulations	3.1 Hotel regulations	
	3.2 Travel agency regulations	
	3.3 Transport regulations	
4 Tourism financing		
5 Tourism policy	5.1 National policy for promoting tourism	
	5.2 Regional tourism policy	5.2.1 Tourism planning
		5.2.2 Environmental protection
	5.3 International tourism policy	5.3.1 Tourism development cooperation
		5.3.2 Ethics of tourism
	5.4 Social tourism policy	
6 Economic monitoring of tourism	6.1 Tourism satellite accounts	
	6.2 Tourism statistics	6.2.1 Tourism balance of payments
		6.2.2 Tourism employment
		6.2.3 Tourism accommodation
		6.2.3.1 Hotels
		6.2.3.2 Open-air accommodation
		...
		6.2.4 Tourism visitor flows
	6.3 Strategy	
	6.4 Forecasting	
7 Tourism actors	7.1 Institutional actors	
	7.2 Professional actors	

3.3 The preparation of the document

Once the classification and shelf-mark system has been defined, each document needs to be shelf-marked and stamped before being stored. Documents for lending should also carry a loan slip held by a plastic pocket glued inside the document. The loan slip should include the following information: the author, title, year of publication and shelf-mark.

An example of a loan slip:

2002	TRAV.ORG.10
BERGER, Jean, The activities of travel agencies in 2001.	
DATE	NAME OF BORROWER

3.4 Making an inventory of the document holdings

By crossing the information of the alphanumerical shelf-mark by subject with the type of document, it becomes possible to keep an inventory of the document holdings. Indeed, this makes it possible to obtain the typology of documents held for each subject in the document holdings. It is also possible to obtain for each type of document the various subjects dealt with. Once the document holdings are digitised, carrying out this work becomes much easier. It then is just a matter of interrogating the field with the relevant shelf-mark at the same time as the specific type of document. For instance, by searching simultaneously for "hotels" in the "shelf-mark" field and for "report" in the "type of document" field, the number of reports relating to hotels can be found.

It is highly recommended to update statistical series regularly concerning the document holdings, as well as the demands made of the Centre and the products and services it offers users, in order to complete successfully such an inventory and to prepare an annual report of the IDRC's activities.

The following information is a proposal of statistics to be updated.

3.5 The list of statistics to be compiled and updated on an annual or monthly basis

The users:

- internal,

- external.

Typology of users: students, teachers, researchers, tourism professionals, tourism companies, tourism institutions, journalists, consultants, interns etc.

The holdings: the number of documents

- Books
- Periodicals
- Case files, dossiers on regulation, clipping files
- Grey literature (documents which are not published or in general circulation)
- Audiovisual documents and CDROMs
- Tourism brochures, maps and guides etc.
- Reference works (dictionaries, atlases, directories etc.)

Acquisitions: the number of documents acquired by

- purchase or by subscription
- exchange
- donation

Documents not held in shelves

- documents on loan (books, journals)
- lost documents

Information processing

- number of analyses carried out and data entry slips entered into the database
- number of dossiers put together and enhanced

The products

The production of the centre: number and nature (reports, directories, newsletters, bibliographies, collections, press reviews, newsletters etc.)

The services provided

- number of questions asked (by type)
- information searches conducted and time taken

- number of selective dissemination profiles

- number of bibliographies and lists compiled on request

- number of photocopies

- number and price of database interrogations

Mail

Volume of mail processed

II.4 PROCESSING AND ANALYSING DOCUMENTS

The process of analysing documents analysis and storing information are among the basic functions of an IDRC as they allow:

- rapid access to information held in databases and to the documents gathered in the documentation centre;

- reference files (catalogues, authority files etc.) and documentary products (referencing bulletins, bibliographies etc.) to be put together.

Three operations are involved in the process of analysing documents:

- bibliographic description
- abstract
- indexing

4.1 The bibliographic description

The bibliographical description or reference (or catalogue entry if the shelf-mark is included) is a compulsory part of analysing documents. It is possible to do without a summary of the document or its indexing (by opting for automatic indexing carried out by the documentation computer programme), but the bibliographical description remains essential. It describes the physical characteristics of the document, independently of its content. This description may be made of all types of documents (texts, images, electronic documents etc.), as well as for extracts of documents.

Bibliographic description has been standardised internationally: the International Standard Book Description (ISBD). The ISBD is a normative document published by the IFLA (International Federation of Library Associations and Institutions) and provides rules for drafting bibliographical descriptions of monographs that can be read with the naked eye or by hand (Braille). The ISBD was first published in 1971, and has been revised four times since (in 1974, 1978, 1987). The writing of a new edition to take into account recommendations relevant to electronic resources began in 2000. Using the ISBD is a means for guaranteeing that bibliographical descriptions are rigorous and faithful, and appropriate for inclusion in library catalogues that cover various types of documents. These bibliographical descriptions may also be exchanged between local, national and international establishments[19].

The ISBD standard brings together all information required for a bibliographic description in 8 specific areas:

1. Title and statement of responsibility area: this area includes the title and name of author(s), and must be filled in.

---

[19] The English ISBD(M) edition of 1987, published by the IFLA, was used by the French Standardisation Association (AFNOR) in drafting its documentation brochure AFNOR Z 44-050, in December 1989, Documentation – Cataloguage des monographes – Rédaction de la description bibliographique.

2. Edition area: it only needs to be filled in if several editions of the same document exist, and is not obligatory.

3. Material (or type of publication) specific area: used for documents that are not books (maps, music scores etc.).

4. Publication, distribution, etc., area: is used for the publisher, place and date of publication.

5. Physical statement description area: draws together information relating to the material characteristics of the document (pagination, format, accompanying material etc.).

6. Series area: the name of the series is put in brackets, and the ISSN (International Standard Serial Number) for serial publication should be included here.

7. Note area: it carries important information which is not included in other zones.

8. Standard number (or alternative) and terms of availability area (ISBN number): it is not obligatory.

Standard model for a catalogue entry includes the bibliographic description plus the shelf-mark of the document (called a catalogue record)?

> Shelf-mark
> Author, first name
> Title: sub-title / Author, second author; translator. – Edition statement. – Place of publication: publisher, date. – Volume number, pages: illustrations; format in centimetres. – (series, number in the series). – Note
> ISBN

The various ISBD areas are cataloguing standards developed mainly for libraries and the presentation of catalogues should respect these standards precisely. Similarly, the punctuation used to separate the areas and information contained in each should be fully respected.

The catalogue record is a model for constituting various catalogues or files. This basic record is copied for each catalogue: the author catalogue, the subject catalogue, the geographical catalogue and the collections catalogue etc.

Documentation centres do not publish catalogues but rather bibliographies, which explains why each centre designs its bibliographic description model according to its needs. Nevertheless, certain general rules must be respected, even if presentations change.

The general entry rules consist of separating the various areas (author, title, address) by ". – " (point, space, dash, space), while the elements within each area are separated by commas. The series is put in brackets[20].

Example of a bibliographic description for monographs

Date   Shelf-mark

AUTHOR, first name. – Title. – Place of publication: publisher,
date. – pagination – (Series)

1960   TOU 25

BERGER, John. – Business travel in Japan: market trends. London: Macmillan, 1960. – 63p. – (Annals)

Example of a bibliographic description for an article

Date

AUTHOR, first name. – Title.
In : Title of periodical, month and/or year, vol., No, p. ...-...

2003

BERGER, John. – Business travel in Japan..
In : Leisure Journal, Oct-Nov 2003, Vol III, No 5, p.240-250.

The creation of various types of catalogues (essential to accessing documents) – also known as heading files or authority files – will not be dealt with here. This is because in a computerised IDRC these various files (called indexes) are created automatically by the documentation software, thus replacing the traditional "cut and paste" which involves reproducing a file several times so that it can be classified in the author catalogue, the titles catalogue etc.

If a manual system is still to be used in the tourism sector, then it is recommended that a subject catalogue dealing with tourism sectors and a geographical catalogue be created, in addition to the catalogues used traditionally in a documentation centre (shelf-mark, author, title).

---

[20] Translator's remark: "parentheses" in American English.

4.2 The abstract

The analysis of a document does not necessarily include an abstract of the document in question and IDRCs do not always have the time and the resources to make summaries. However, even a few succinct lines on the contents of a document are often enough to enrich a bibliographic description.

There are several types of abstract, of which the three main ones are:

The indicative abstract: it generally includes the main chapter titles and headings of the document, linked to each other by terms like "first", "next", "then", "lastly". This abstract is only made up of a few lines and remains wholly impersonal.

The informative abstract: it is more developed, and requires a real analysis and summary. It is used to provide hard information about the content of the document and may even substitute for reading the document. It is aimed at experts, and may be a page long.

The selective abstract: it selects information according to the category of user and modifies the balance of the text by only presenting certain aspects.

The three types of abstract may be used in an IDRC for tourism, depending on the relevance of the document. For brochures and promotional documents an indicative abstract may be used, whereas for studies or research documents an informative abstract can be used to draw out the main ideas of the author. For more general documents, which may include only a few chapters on tourism, a selective abstract is appropriate etc.

> The abstract should allow the reader to decide whether the document meets his/her needs.

4.3 Indexing

The aim of indexing is to facilitate the search for documents in the database or document holdings in order to answer to questions. It involves describing and characterising a document using the representations of concepts contained in the document, in other words to transcribe, using a indexing language, concepts extracted from the document by analysis. The transcription in indexing language is carried out using indexing tools like thesauruses, lexicons or lists of keywords etc[21].

In other words, the aim is to extract concepts from the document which describe its content as completely as possible, then to select the most pertinent concepts which have been chosen and the most specific, relating to the description of the document's

---
21 AFNOR Z-47-102

subject(s). Lastly, the selected concepts need to be translated into an indexing language using a thesaurus, a lexicon or a keyword list. For tourism, the World Tourism Organisation's Multilingual Thesaurus on Tourism and Leisure Activities may be used.

Indexing is an obligatory part of the process of analysing documents. It is carried out in two stages.

The extraction of meaningful terms from the text is done using the same elements as the abstract, i.e. from the title, the table of contents, the introduction, the preface and the publisher's summary. The person indexing the document should pay attention to the rules of "selectiveness", "completeness", and "specificity".

The semantic transformation of meaningful terms involves their translation into an indexing language. This means validating relevant terms. This may be done by using the Multilingual Thesaurus on Tourism and Leisure Activities in the following way:

a) Does the concept exist in the thesaurus? If "yes", then ensure that it is a descriptor, in other words a term which may be employed in indexing, and not a synonym. It should also be checked whether the term is a reference for other descriptors, its relevance verified and then the document can be indexed.

b) If the concept does not exist in the thesaurus, then the closest equivalent in the list should be found, its relevance verified, and then the document can be indexed.

Automatic indexing

There are now computer programmes available which can automatically classify and index documents. However, such documents need to be digitised, and readable on screen. It is also possible for documents to be indexed on the basis of their abstracts. Automatic indexing may be controlled by using a dictionary of empty words which lists terms that should not be indexed (articles, prepositions, adverbs, verbs etc.), but it may also be controlled by the obligatory use of a thesaurus.

Whatever IT system may be used, the process of analysing a document (bibliographic description, abstract, indexing) will require using a coding sheet.

4.4 The coding sheet

In a computerised IDRC, the bibliographic descriptions are put on coding sheets or processing slips. These were presented in the first part of this handbook. Here, further information is given about the areas of the coding sheet (and the data entry form) of a bibliographic reference, areas which are useful for an IDRC on tourism. In the case of computerised holdings, all the areas may be interrogated and all generate their own index.

Type of document	Shelf-mark	ISBN/ISSN/ISRN
Title		
Name of periodical	No of periodical	Series
Volume	Pagination	Language
Sponsoring org.	Physical author	Corporate author
Publisher	Place Date of publication	Number of copies
Abstract		
Subject descriptor		
Access to document		Geographic descriptor
Person responsible for data entry		Place of consultation
Evaluation		Date of entry

Type of document: it is worth entering data for this area as it allows searches to be made according to the exact typology of documents. It is also used to provide an inventory of the document holdings at any moment.

Shelf-mark: if an alphanumerical shelf-mark is used by sector of tourism activity in this area, then interrogating the area will indicate the number of documents relating to a specific subject.

Name of periodical: this area is to be filled in for articles. The index created for this area enables a large list of tourism press and research titles to be compiled.

Language: a search on this areas shows how many documents are available in each language.

Sponsoring organisation: this area needs to be filled in when, for example, the Tourism Administration commissions a study or report from a consultant or researcher. The area makes it possible to establish an inventory of documents commissioned by the NTA or by other organisations.

Author: this is a physical person as opposed to the corporate author which is an organisation. The recommended presentation is: Name, first name. This allows an alphabetical list of authors in the field of tourism to be drawn up.

Corporate author: It is recommended to enter the name in capital letters, to avoid acronyms and to use the full name of the organisation, unless the acronym is better known (e.g. UNESCO).

Date: an entry for this area is obligatory. If the exact date is not known, it is necessary to find an approximate date, followed by a question mark (e.g. 2001?).

Number of copies (printed): this area may be useful in managing stocks of publications by the NTA.

Subject descriptor: this is the indexing field of the keywords chosen from the Thesaurus on Tourism and Leisure Activities.

Geographic descriptor: uses the above-mentioned thesaurus for indexing.

Access to document: this area allows the profile of users to be defined and to manage confidentiality.

Place of consultation: this area may be useful if documents or part of the Centre's documents can be consulted in other places.

Evaluation: this area allows the relevance of documents or categories of documents to be evaluated, using a pre-established grid.

II.5 RETRIEVING INFORMATION

To meet the demand for information, the information manager carries out searches. These may concern the document holdings of the National Tourism Administration. But they may also relate to specialised computer information databases, both public and private. Lastly, they can cover the greatest database throughout the world, namely Internet. The aim of this handbook is not to deal with research methodology for different types of library files of catalogues, which is also known as "manual search", nor so-called "free-text search" (natural language), for which search tools are not yet fully operational and effective. The advice which follows is geared to helping the reader carry out search and retrieval by using computer systems.

5.1 Information search with the help of the *Thesaurus on Tourism and Leisure Activities*

The goal of processing the document holdings by elaborating record sheets and bibliographic descriptions is to be able to carry out searches on the computerised holdings and so to meet the requests for information by internal and external users. As the databases are indexed using the WTO's thesaurus, the same search language (the same thesaurus[22]) will obviously be used for retrieving information.

The multilingual (English, French, Spanish and Italian) Thesaurus on Tourism and Leisure Activities[23,] includes for each language more than 2000 terms, descriptors and non-descriptors (synonyms). It is organised into 20 semantic fields, with a maximum of five levels of hierarchy. For each language, the Thesaurus provides:

A structured alphabetical list: this is the key element of the Thesaurus. All the descriptors and non-descriptors are listed here, with their relationships, notes of usage or definition, and the subject category to which each is allocated.

The descriptors are printed in bold characters, followed by the linguistic equivalent, the Micro-Thesaurus number and the scope note (where one exists), any non-descriptors, the broader term, the immediate narrower terms, and lastly any associated descriptors when such relationship is judged to be useful. The non-descriptors are presented in italics and in small letters.

A hierarchical list: this gives the descriptors organised in 20 semantic fields, according to their hierarchical level. The latter is indicated by numbers, which allow descriptors at the same level of hierarchy to be presented in the same column.

A list of descriptor groups (micro-thesaurus): for each semantic field, this list presents groups of descriptors and non-descriptors. Its function is to present the general

---

22 A structured list of standardised terms organised in a hierarchy, which makes it possible, on the one hand, to describe the content of a piece of information, and on the other hand, to retrieve information by subject. As a common and dynamic language between the database producer and users, this tool offers the possibility of inserting, modifying or deleting a concept at any time.

23 The first Italian edition of the Thesaurus on Tourism and Leisure Activities was published by the University of Lecce in 2003. The Portuguese version prepared under the aegis of the General Directorate for Tourism of Portugal as well as the Croatian version prepared by the Zagreb Institute for Tourism should become available in 2004.

structure of the Thesaurus in its first two levels of hierarchy. The classification is of an indicative nature and is not designed to be adopted for the classification of documents. The descriptors are preceded by a triple, two-digit serial number which allows the classification to be the same in all the linguistic versions of the Thesaurus. The first two-digit number of the serial number is that of the semantic field in which the descriptor is classified. The descriptor at the top of the group is the broadest term, and is indicated by bold type.

A permuted list: this list allows the alphabetic transcription of all the component words of a descriptor or non-descriptor. It presents each key word in its context (KWIC or KeyWord in Context).

Advice on searches: formulating questions with the help of a thesaurus

The conceptual formulation of questions required to retrieve information is similar to indexing a document. However, this process is different because it must define the concepts contained in the questions, concepts that are likely to be found in the documents available. These concepts must then be converted into descriptors, which are subsequently used to retrieve the documents from the database.

The steps for searching in the database are as follows:

1. A question is formulated using the following descriptor: TOURIST CONSUMPTION.

   Entering this descriptor allows all documents relating to this subject to be retrieved or extracted from the file.

2. Several descriptors may be used to formulate a more specific question. They can be linked using "Boolean operators": AND, OR, NOT, for example:

   TOURIST CONSUMPTION **AND** OECD COUNTRIES
   Only documents which relate to both terms will be selected.

   TOURIST CONSUMPTION **OR** OECD COUNTRIES
   All documents which relate to either term will be selected.

   TOURIST CONSUMPTION **NOT** OECD COUNTRIES
   All documents which related to tourist consumption but not to consumption in the OECD countries will be selected.

3. For more complex research equations, descriptors may be grouped together in brackets. Such brackets have the same significance as they do in mathematics.

   TOURIST CONSUMPTION **AND** HOLIDAYS **NOT** (OFF-PEAK HOLIDAYS **AND** EUROPEANS ON HOLIDAY)

Flow Chart for Using a Theasurus

START

Select a word or an expression relating to the information search (if there are several, the procedure must be repeated for each)

↓

Consult the alphabetical list of descriptors and non-descriptors

↓ ↓

- The word is listed
  - The word is a descriptor → Note it down
  - The word is not a descriptor → Note down the descriptor given by USE
- The word is not listed
  - Consult the permuted list to see if the word or part of the expression is given as part of a descriptor, then note the descriptor.

↓

Consult the descriptor's semantic field to see if a more relevant descriptor exists

↓

Interrogate the holdings : there are 3 possibilities

↓ ↓ ↓

- The number and quality of references is satisfactor
- There are too few references (silence) → Expand the search with a BT and/or RT or by using another descriptor, preceded by OR
- There are too many references (noise) → Specify the search either with an NT, or by using another descriptor preceded by AND or NOT.

↓

END

Lebreton/Pérés

5.2 Exploring the Internet Network

5.2.1 Basic steps for surfing the Internet

Hypertext links

Hypertext links make it possible to surf the Internet, by allowing users to move from one site to another. Such links may be associated with a word, a sentence or an image. When the (mouse) cursor passes over a link, its presentation changes from an "arrow" to a "hand". Links are often in blue (or in another colour compared to the rest of the text) and they are generally underlined. Clicking on the mouse's left button is all that is need to activate a link (and so move to the Internet page it refers to).

There are two main types of links:

- "Internal" links, which are used to move to another point within the same site,

- "External" links, which move to another site.

Lastly, some links allow files to be downloaded (but care should be taken in doing this due to viruses such files may contain).

Internet addresses

Given the ease of surfing on Internet and moving from one site to anther, it is useful to know where one is, using a URL address, which is indicated at the top of the screen.

URL stands for *Uniform Resource Locator*, and indicates exactly the location of a file on the Internet, as well as the means to access it. For an address like http://www.education.gouv.fr :

- http stands for Hyper Text Transfer Protocol,

- ://www is the path indicating that the server is on the World Wide Web,

- education the name of the organisation or company,

- gouv.fr is the suffix indicating the country or activity (or both).

The services offered

The following is a typology of information and communication services relevant to tourism:

- Communication: international electronic messaging, discussion forums, information letters,

- Scientific publications: electronic journals, pre-publications, research reports, conference proceedings,

- Documentary reference services: library catalogues, bibliographical databases and full-text, intelligence products,

- Administrative information: calls for tenders, conference enrolments, directories, biographies, annual reports.

5.2.2 Information retrieval and access strategies

To carry out a search on Internet, it is vital to know what the various categories of search tools are and how to use them in order to chose the most relevant function for the search. The tools presented here are merely a sample of some of the main functions which can be used on Internet. It is a minimal selection as the available supply is vast. Further information is available on professional or specialised sites, at the end of the chapter.

5.2.3 Directories

Directories seek out sites. Searches are undertaken by selecting categories, subjects, sub-subjects. Only the titles and categories are indexed in directories. Referenced sites are indexed at the demand of the site creator.

Key French-speaking directories include:

- YAHOO: http://fr.yahoo.com

- NOMADE: http://www.nomade.tiscali.fr

- VOILA: http://www.voila.fr

- LYCOS: http://www.lycos.fr

The main English-speaking directories include:

- YAHOO: http://www.yahoo.com

- MAGELLAN: http://www.mckinley.com which classifies, indexes and provides a description of sites.

- OPEN DIRECTORY: http://open-directory.com

- EBLAST: http://www.eblast.com produced by the Encyclopaedia Britannica, which provides a directory of 125 000 Internet sites, selected for their contents.

- WEBCRAWLER: http://www.webcrawler.com

Apart from these generalist sites, which identify and classify sites for the general and professional public in all areas of information, many specific and subject-based directories also exist:

INVISIBLE-WEB.NET: http://www.invisible-web.net indicates the best sources of the invisible Web (that is to say approximately 550 billion documents which are not indexed by search engines etc.).

TOORISTA: http://www.toorista.com is specialised in travel.

There are also some selective directories in the field of education: http://www.lii.org (*Librarian's Index to the Internet* which presents 11000 sites accessible by category), http://www.ipl.org (*The Internet Public Library*, created by the University of Michigan, displays 20000 entries), http://www.academicinfo.net (Academic Info), http://www.infomine.ucr.edu (Infomine is managed by a network of university libraries and describes 111000 sites) and lastly http://www.digital.library.upenn.edu/books (The Online Books Page which is a directory of sites providing access to digitised publications).

5.2.4 Search engines

These are robots which search pages on the web and which index the full text of pages in order to develop a database that may be interrogated using a simple search form or a complex form with Boolean operators and an on-line help function.
The most-used search engines are:

- GOOGLE: http://www.google.com
- ALTA VISTA: http://www.altavista.com
- ALL THE WEB : http://www.alltheweb.com

5.2.5 Metamotors

They do not prospect the Internet and do not generate databases, but allow several search engines to be interrogated at the same time. Indeed, given that no single search engine covers the web entirely, it is necessary to interrogate several to obtain a panorama of what actually exists on the Internet for a certain subject. Metamotors allow simultaneous interrogation of several directories and generalist search engines. This is true for http://www.metacrawler.com or http://www.kartoo.com, which interrogate 14 directories and motors, including Google, Alta Vista, All the Web, Webcrawler, Yahoo, Nomade and Voila. Metamotors also exist to interrogate the invisible web, such as http://www.profusion.com and http://www.queryserver.com.

Using a metamotor is useful when first tackling a subject to obtain rapidly the most relevant documents selected by various robots and directories. However, it is less advisable to use metamotors for acquiring exhaustive information about a subject, or if the subject is complex.

5.2.6 Intelligent agents and intelligence search on Internet

A "agent" is defined as an entity which has its own logical capacity, or "intelligence", acting on behalf of someone else.

Characteristics

Four characteristics distinguish such agents from the other search tools presented above:

- Autonomy: they must take initiative and act without interference by users. They must be able to carry out a search on Internet even when the user is disconnected.

- A capacity to communicate and to cooperate: they must be able to exchange information with other agents or servers and integrate new demands by users.

- A capacity to reason and react: they must be capable of adapting permanently to their environment.

- Mobility: they should be able to navigate through different IT architectures and software etc.

Agents are therefore programmes for searching information which have the capacity to carry out tasks automatically, in place of users.

Functions

Intelligent agents execute several tasks in the following manner:

- Searching for information: most agent programmes are based on a metamotor which interrogates several search engines simultaneously. The number of search engines varies, ranging from dozens to hundreds. It is often possible to add extra sources from a list proposed by the programme.

- A cartographic analysis: it should specify and provide perspective to the results obtained.

- Statistical and semantic analysis: this involves studying the information found through the automatic indexing of results or the drafting of a summary.

- Filtering: it consists of removing repeat results, obsolescent links and unwanted pages.

- Tracking and updating: this is based on visiting selected sites regularly (the periodicity may be set by the user) in order to identify changes to these sites and new, relevant pages.

- Archiving: allows the information obtained to be edited and stored.

- Off-line consultation: selected sites and pages are downloaded to be consulted locally.

Typology

Given these tasks, an attempt may be made to classify intelligent agents:

- Monitoring agents: they monitor websites or specific subjects of interest. They can be used to be automatically alerted about the latest news of choice: Webspector, BullsEye, Website-Watcher, Digimind Monitor.

- Search agents: Copernic, Strategic Finder, Webseeker.

- Offline browsers or information extractors: eCatch, Teleport Pro, NetVigie all allow the contents (entirely or in part) of a site to be downloaded.

- Intelligence portals: these are strategic tools, like Autonomy, OpenPortal4U or V-Strat, which have several modules which that intelligence to be collected, stored, analysed and disseminated.

The URL addresses of all these agents and many others can be found on the Agentland site (see below).

The use of intelligent agents is especially recommended for frequent and complete updating of data on specific subjects. They may also be used by information managers who carry out intelligence gathering, notably on Internet, either for a specific user or to compile information newsletters with news and intelligence on a certain sector. It should be noted, however, that these tools are not substitutes for traditional intelligence and do not replace more conventional methods of searching for information on Internet. (Further information about intelligence techniques and possibilities may be found in directories specifically dedicated to this.)

5.2.7 Internet directories for intelligence gathering

To expand such information it is possible to use professional and specialised sites such as:

- http://www.adbs.fr (French site for information professionals),

- http://www.veille.com (a professional site for finding strategic business intelligence),

- http://www.agentland.com ; this is a portal of intelligent agents. More than 450 agents are referenced and assessed. They may be downloaded from this site.

There are also guides to intelligence gathering on the Internet:

Competitive intelligence: http://www.fuld.com is conducted by Fuld&Company, a private American company specialised in the field of business intelligence since 1979. The Internet Intelligence Index on its website lists more than 600 Internet sites carrying out intelligence gathering.

The CI Resource Index: http://www.ciseek.com references more than 1670 sites in the field of intelligence, classified by category and sub-category.

II.6 CREATING AND DISTRIBUTING DOCUMENTARY PRODUCTS

The chapter dealing with the creation of the document holdings sets out the various types of documents held and their typology. Documentary products fall into the secondary and tertiary categories of documents. Their creation is the raison d'être of the IDRC, as they allow the Centre to disseminate and make available the information it has collected and processed.

The present chapter outlines the main products which the IDRC of the National Tourism Administration should create.

6.1 Files or dossiers

6.1.1 Case files or documentary dossiers

Case files or documentary dossiers draw together documents on a particular subject. The documents are taken from various sources and may vary in form and support. For the IDRC of a NTA, two types of case files are necessary:

- working files or dossiers

- customised files or dossiers.

Working files or dossiers handle a specific subject, often of current interest, and which is permanently in demand by users. They provide updated information on the subject, and relieve the information manager from answering the same questions repeatedly. Such files need to be regularly updated and old information withdrawn. They may be kept in folders or hanging files. Working files or dossiers can also be classified. They are to be consulted in the IDRC and should not be lent out.

Customised files or dossiers are created at the specific request of a user. Such files are not updated, but they may be used as the basis of a working file.

6.1.2 Clipping files

This type of file much resembles the case files, but it is distinguished by the fact that it only includes press clippings. Clipping files aim to address current affairs issues, and need to be regularly updated, with old clippings discarded. Their lifespan may be short, but they may be preserved for historical interest.

6.1.3 Dossiers on laws and regulations

There is much demand for this type of dossier within the NTA. They include information on all stages in the development of legislation and legal regulations: parliamentary bills, parliamentary reports and debates. Once a bill has been voted into law, all commentaries and summaries relating to the law have to be collected and preserved. These dossiers provide the essential information on laws and regulations in the tourism sector, for example, travel and hotels.

6.2 Lists, directories and compendiums

The IDRC may also put together various directories and lists on tourism. However, there are two main subjects an IDRC specialised in tourism must develop: directories or lists of the actors involved in this sector and compendiums on legislation affecting tourism.

6.2.1 Directories or lists of tourism professionals

This type of information is greatly in demand in the tourism sector, which has a very diverse set of actors. The exact choice of lists to be compiled depends on the demands made of the IDRC. The following is a suggestion of lists of tourism actors to be established:

A. The national organisation of tourism
   Ministries – Parliament
   National Tourism Administration (NTA) and related organisations
   Regional Tourism Directorates
   Overseas Tourism Departments

B. The regional organisation of tourism
   Regional Tourism Committees
   Local Tourism Committees
   Tourist Offices (regional and local federations)
   Chambers of Commerce and Industry
   Economic Monitoring Organisations (national and regional)

C. The organisation of tourism abroad
   Foreign, National Tourism Administrations
   National Statistics Institutes
   Embassies
   Foreign Tourist Offices
   Foreign Chambers of Commerce

D. The international organisation of tourism
   International Tourism Organisations
   International Organisations providing and collecting statistical information

E. Training, education and research in tourism
    Tourism trades and vocational training
    Employment and Recruitment
    Universities providing education in tourism
    Research organisations
    National Organisations providing and collecting information

F. Tourism industries
    Hotels and hotel chains
    Outdoor accommodation – camping
    Rental holiday homes – bed & breakfast – home exchanges
    Non-profit-making tourism – subsidised accommodation
    Time sharing accommodation
    Travel agencies – tour operators
    Tourism associations
    Catering – gastronomy
    Transport (air transport, maritime transport, rail transport, road transport)
    Trade fairs

G. Tourism and leisure activities
    Sports and leisure activities
    Yachting and river cruising
    Leisure parks
    Fishing – hunting
    Business tourism – congresses – casinos
    Coach tourism
    Cultural and religious tourism (cultural heritage, cultural activities, religious tourism)
    Garden tourism
    Tourism for the disabled
    Health tourism – spa tourism – thalassotherapy
    Maritime tourism – maritime and river cruises
    Nature tourism and trekking (hiking, long-distance riding, bicycle touring)
    Senior tourism
    Youth tourism – language stays

H. Tourism areas
    Tourism and the environment
    Rural areas – rural tourism
    Coastlines – coastal tourism
    Mountains – mountain tourism
    Urban areas – urban tourism
    Natural parks

I. Tourist information and documentation
Consumer protection
Information and/or reservation services
Documentation centres specialised in tourism
Tourist press (main serial publications dedicated to tourism, information and promotion newsletters)
Professional guides (general directories, subject directories)
Tourism engineering and consulting organisations

6.2.2 Compendium of legal texts

All professional sectors within the tourism industry deal permanently with laws and regulations governing their activities: e.g. several steps have to be taken when opening a hotel or a travel agency, requiring a good knowledge of existing legislation. It is therefore vital for the IDRC to assemble a compendium of the main texts that are the basis of tourist activities and tourism organisations, and which regulate them. The following is a suggested list of such texts:

A. Legal texts relating to tourism institutions
- International tourism institutions: world organisations, regional inter-governmental institutions and non-governmental organisations.
- National tourism institutions: the public organisation of tourism, the national administration of tourism, the territorial organisation of tourism.

B. Legal texts regulating the various tourism professions and industries
- Travel: travel agencies, tour operators, not-for-profit associations, e-tourism, transport etc.
- Tourism accommodation: accommodation standards, accommodation contracts, services etc.
- Tour guides

C. Legal texts relating to the development and protection of tourism sites
- Rural areas
- Coastlines
- Mountains
- Natural parks and nature reserves

6.3 Technical sheets and methodological guides

The technical sheets and methodologies may be produced in the field of documentation techniques and new information technologies when the IDRC of the Tourism Administration plays a leading role in the information and documentation policy within the Tourist Authority, *vis-à-vis* other documentation centres and units that it supervises.

These technical sheets allow working methods to be standardised, in order to develop documentary products, booklets, data coding sheets etc. They may also guide users in using Internet, electronic messaging etc.

6.4 Summary reports

These reports outline existing knowledge, at any given moment, on a specific subject. They save users from consulting large quantities of documents. Such reports should be drafted by information managers who have a very good knowledge of the sector, and should be checked by a specialist of the field in question. The reports provide updated knowledge, using research, analysis and contacts with professionals. They may also be developed for questions relating to the law on tourism (see below), as well as relating to sectoral aspects of tourism. This type of product greatly enhances the reputation of the Centre.

6.5 Annual report

The annual report of the Centre's activities is an essential document as it is not just a way for evaluating the services provided by the IDRC, but it is also an important means for stressing the fundamental, logistical role the Centre plays within the NTA. The report is easy to compile using the statistics updated throughout the year, which is indeed another reason for keeping such statistics up to date.

The report should include the following items:

A presentation of the IDRC: its year of creation, staff, position in the organisation chart, means of functioning and changes which occurred during the year relating to the Centre's organisation, its personnel, premises and material.

The presentation should also include the precise situation of the staff, their level of training and the training courses followed.

An analysis of its administrative activities: these are the daily functions of the IDRC, relating to such tasks as management of mail, photocopying, secretarial services, mailing of documents etc. The Centre's budget should also be presented.

An analysis of the Centre's technical documentary activities. These can be set out in several tables:

- A table setting out the demand for information which is addressed to the Centre, with a typology of users and a typology of requests and searches undertaken. Internal and external demand should be distinguished, and whether requests arrive by mail, email, telephone etc.

- A table setting out the document holdings and its evolution (new acquisitions during the year, rise in the volume and type of documents, an assessment of subscriptions (number and cost) and development of the databases.

- Products completed and distributed: the type, number and different networks of recipients.

- Services provided: the type and number (photocopies, document scans, documents posted on the Internet or Intranet sites etc.).

The presentation of specific activities

It is important to estimate the time spent on specific, more promotional activities, such as the organisation of exhibitions, open-days, the preparation of activity assessments, co-productions with other partners, the participation in library networks or discussion groups on Internet, training and the maintenance of competencies.

Participation in a partnership network

The report should mention all joint activities with the Centre's institutional and professional partners. It should also include meetings organised by the Centre within the Tourism Administration, or meetings in which it has participated. Any participation in working parties should also be covered (e.g. on Internet, new technologies, specific tourism dossiers etc.). The Centre's involvement in major events must also figure: press conferences, professional trade fairs, conferences or seminars on tourism.

Training activities

Apart from specific training activities organised by the IDRC, the annual report should mention and quantify each time the Centre's staff provide technical or methodological support to the personnel in other departments, in the use of databases, software, multimedia or Internet searches.

Projects to be developed

The annual report also provides a good opportunity for the Centre to compare its activities over the year with those of previous years, to draw conclusions, and to put forward new propositions or announce new projects to be developed.

6.6 Catalogues and bibliographies

The catalogue is the instrument used to identify and locate documents which make up the holdings. It includes all the bibliographic entries of the IDRC. As for a bibliography, it is the most common product distributed by the IDRC. Its aim is to alert readers of the arrival of new documents or the publication of new information. It allows information to be identified during selection. Once the document holdings are computerised, this type of document may be edited automatically by carrying out simple searches on the database. A current bibliography is produced to indicate new acquisitions by the Centre. A subject or selective bibliography may be compiled to meet a specific request. A bibliography is retrospective when going back several years, and it may be analytical if the documents indicated carry an analytical summary.

6.7 Press reviews and press tables of contents reviews

These involve the selection, presentation and release of articles. Press reviews may be daily, or weekly. They may be generalist or specialist, or both at the same time (in which case they include clippings from the general press and the tourism trade press). Putting together press reviews may be time-consuming and fastidious, if the IDRC lacks resources. It may also be useful to provide reviews of tables of contents, which present tables of contents taken from the trade press, especially from journals received by the Centre. Such reviews should include a table allowing users to order articles they are interested in. Photocopies of the latter can then be sent to users.

6.8 Electronic products

The advent of new information technologies has completely transformed the process of producing and distribution tourism products. Ever more sophisticated software provides the possibilities of editing all forms of bibliographies and newsletters, with just a few "clicks". Full-text documents can be presented and emailed thanks to electronic document management. Similarly, it is also possible to create press reviews automatically using scanning equipment.

Internet and electronic mail are two new tools which allow the IDRC's output to be distributed in the international information market. Once these have been structured and put into place, these information supports can spare the Centre all costs associated with paper publishing. They can play a crucial role in boosting the Centre's image, as well as providing unprecedented interactivity. When the Centre receives a request for information by email, for example, it is possible for the information manager to put together an automatically-edited bibliography and send it back to the user within a few minutes. The latter may then return an email, indicating documents of particular interest. If these documents are digitised, they can then be sent immediately to the user. Hence, an IDRC in Africa may handle extensively a request for information emanating from Australia.

6.8.1 Creating an Internet site

Generally speaking, an IDRC is not responsible for creating the Internet site of the National Tourism Administration. This task normally falls to the Communication service/department of the NTA. However, the IDRC should participate actively in the steering committee of the project, due to its professional competencies in information gathering and processing. In case the IDRC is responsible for the site, software for creating and managing a website is now available, which does not require the knowledge of the HTML programming language. Products like "Dreamweaver" or "Frontpage" can be used, following a short training course. They allow web pages to be created and modified, which include (moving) images.

6.8.2 The Intranet: a documentary information portal

Intranet is the portal par excellence for documentary information, and has miraculous capacities for interconnecting administrative structures which are usually partitioned and little connected.

What is Intranet?

An Intranet consists in using Internet technology to create an IT network within an organisation. Indeed, Internet is not only a rapid means of communication with the whole world, but it is also a way of optimising internal communication within an organisation, as it permits more efficient networking than do traditional networks.

Why use Intranet?

Developing and using an Intranet server within a Tourism Administration is part of a general policy and strategy to have modern and effective internal communication. The goal is to use the knowledge, experience and know-how existent within the administration more profitably, in as far as Intranet allows all departments to work jointly on common projects. This should facilitate and shorten decision-making processes. The aim of Intranet is thus:

- to facilitate access to current information and reference documents which are regularly updated;

- to cut time needed to access information;

- to enlarge the scope of information available to management and personnel;

- to draw together information, leading to a single point of entry;

- to share information: important sources of strategic information exist in the various departments of the Authority and these should be made available to all, in a structured manner that allows them to be identified rapidly;

- to modernise the ways and methods of working (interactivity, group working, sharing resources, procedures and applications etc.);

- to improve the quality of services and their effectives, while cutting costs.

Who is Intranet used by?

This work tool is at everybody's disposal within the NTA, but should also be open to decentralised and regional offices of the administration, to organisations under the Authority's supervision and to the overseas offices of the Administration. It may be used as the homepage on the computers of all personnel.

What is the content of Intranet?

The content of Intranet should be set by a steering committee organised and run by the IDRC, the Communication Service/Department and the IT Department. This committee remains responsible for the content of the Intranet and the information presented on it. Several categories of information can be identified:

- institutional information: changes in policy, institutional reforms and structural modifications;

- strategic information: sectoral information, be it transversal or geographic, contained in working papers and which is vital to decision-making: reference texts, statistical data, documents being prepared, as well as forecasts,

- information about human resources: employment, careers, training;

- practical information: schedules (missions, business trips, meetings etc.), bookings of meeting rooms and equipment;

- communication: emails, classified ads, discussion forums, working groups.

6.8.3 Intranet as a portal for the IDRC

The IDRC may participate in developing and updating the various sections of the Tourism Administration's Intranet. But it could also have its own Intranet portal to serve the Centre's users. This could become a real instrument for presenting both the Centre's databases and its documentary products: compendium of laws and regulations on tourism, directories of professional actors and experts, on-line press reviews and analytical bibliographies of tourism activities, case files and sectoral summaries, directories of Internet sites useful to tourism, mailing lists, current affairs dossiers, forms for requesting documents, subscriptions, forms requesting the selective dissemination of information or intelligence search in a specific area etc. Such information is obviously presented in a structured manner, with sections broken down in a harmonious, user-friendly way.

Newsletters and intelligence via email

To launch a newsletter, it is first necessary to set up an intelligence gathering system. This will be studied in the following chapter.

II.7 ORGANISING INTELLIGENCE GATHERING

The principles, definitions and various forms of intelligence gathering were discussed in the first part of this handbook. Such intelligence gathering in the field of tourism is presented here, using the specific example of an electronic newsletter. This allows the successive stages in intelligence gathering to be described and to set out the organisation of each step and the operations needed to be put into place.

Creating an electronic documentary intelligence information newsletter on Internet, in the field of tourism

The aim of this newsletter is to inform members of the information network about current economic news in the tourism sector.

As with all information and documentation products, the newsletter must be designed to meet users' actual needs and/or potential demands. It is thus constructed in response to the network of its recipients. The newsletter is a generalist product of interest to all actors in the world of tourism and tourism education.

Various steps are taken in establishing the newsletter.

7.1 Building up an intelligence gathering network

The IDRC may use its own address book as well as other existing tourism directories in order to build up a network of correspondents. Directories of tourism actors can be constituted according to their functions and the typology of tourism professions. This will allow selected information to be sent out to particular groups. These directories are created in the electronic address books of software managing email (e.g. Netscape, MS Outlook etc.). The mailing list may be broken down into groups and sub-groups as follows:

The National Tourism Administration
    Organisations under State supervision
    Offices in foreign countries
    Regional and local offices of the National Tourism Administration

The network of institutional actors in tourism
    National organisations and associations of tourism professionals
    Regional and local organisations
    Chambers of Commerce
    National and regional statistics organisations
    Other ministries and administrations involved in tourism
    Foreign tourist offices

Education network
    Research organisations and laboratories
    Tourism universities
    Tourism schools
    Vocational training organisations

Press networks
    Tourism trade press

International networks
    International tourism organisations
    International organisations acting in areas related to tourism (UNEP, WHO, ILO etc.)
    International statistics organisations

Networks of tourism professionals
    Hotels and catering
    Travel services
    Transport companies
    Congress and trade-fair organisers
    Sport and leisure activity organisers
    Developers and promoters of tourist regions and resorts (rural, coastline, mountain and urban tourism)
    Consultants
    Organisations of tourist information and documentation

7.2 Creating the electronic newsletter

7.2.1 The layout

Designing the layout, its structure and its graphic presentation can be sub-contracted to an outside company specialised in creating newsletters. But if the IDRC does not have the necessary finance, it is still possible to design a layout internally, with some help from the NTA's IT department. Software exists which allows such publications to be designed fairly easily. The model for the newsletter may be created in PDF format and sent as an attachment to an email. But it could also be created in Microsoft Word, whose more recent versions allow HTML pages to be created, or indeed in Netscape, using the "Composer" function.

7.2.2 The contents of the newsletter

Once the networks receiving the newsletter have been created and their needs identified, it is possible to develop the contents and various sections of the newsletter.

The following is a list of possible sections:

- News about the Tourism Administration: this section provides information about, and promotes the activities of the various departments of the National Tourism Administration for outside correspondents. It also informs the personnel of the Authority about current activities.

- Research: a research section is a way of disseminating development in tourism research: publications and work in progress, congresses, conferences and seminars. New research teams and units can also be presented.

- International tourism: focuses on international events affecting the evolution of tourism. It presents the international market and may be broken down by country, indicating tourist flows and behaviour.

- Environment: this section provides all information relating to the development of tourism regions and sites and the protection of the environment. It provides information about all forms of sustainable development which may affect tourism.

- Economic monitoring and analysis: relates to the national tourism market, its specificities, its trends, the international economy and national policies which may have an impact on tourism and its development. The section also covers forecasting.

- Events: indicates national and international events organised for and by tourism professionals.

- Public administration: This section provides information about State policy in the field of tourism, as well as any other type of information which may be of interest to public employees working in tourism (wages, pensions etc.).

- Information technology: identifies all forms of new technology that could be useful to the tourism sector, whether it concerns ticketing, reservation systems or e-tourism. New Internet sites dedicated to tourism can also be presented.

- Tourism laws and regulations: indicates and discusses all new laws and regulations affecting the tourism sector, along with commentaries published in various articles and other publications.

- Documentation: this sector indicates new publications acquired by the IDRC and other works released in the field of tourism. Books and articles may be simply indicated, but its is better to include presentations or abstracts.

7.2.3 Internal and external Internet links

External links are created to indicate the sources of documents which have been selected on Internet.

Internal links are used within the document to navigate between sections or between items of information. For example, if a piece of information falls into several categories, such as an international event relating to the environment, then internal links within the newsletter may be used to refer to both sections in the newsletter.

7.3 Organising intelligence gathering within the IDRC

All members of the IDRC's staff should participate in intelligence gathering. The various sections of the newsletter should each have their own in-tray in the Centre, so that all documents received by the Centre can be easily and immediately classified. All information arriving at the IDRC, whatever its form, support and origin, should be classified like this, before being processed further. A pre-selection can then be made of information to be included in the newsletter and which can be later discarded. Such information tends to have a short shelf-life (announcements of events, documents relating to the political, social and economic outlook etc.). The other type of information concerns documents that are presented in the newsletter, and which are then preserved in the document holdings. A bibliographic description will subsequently be made of such documents and integrated into the Centre's database. This is the case for acquisitions by the Centre (orders, subscriptions, exchanges etc.) and for all grey literature.

The IDRC staff should also be in permanent contact with the other departments or the Tourist Authority in order to provide information for the "News about the National Tourism Administration" (NTA) section. Each department could designate someone responsible for informing the Centre about activities and news to be presented. An email can also be sent out to all departmental contacts or heads during the drafting of the newsletter.

7.4 Organising intelligence gathering on the Internet

Intelligence gathering on Internet involves several steps: searching for information, collecting, assessing, selecting, checking and processing it. Some of these steps may be automated, for example, searching and collecting information. This helps make time available for checking and processing information collected.

7.4.1 Searching on the Internet

Once the needs of the newsletter have been defined and its sections created, searching for information starts by identifying and locating formal and informal sources of information on the Internet: casual sources, professional networks, partner sites, information providers (the press, libraries, servers and information brokers, databases, information centres), institutions, consultants and experts, events etc.

Traditional search tools are used to do this, such as search engines or metamotors.

7.4.2 Creating a directory of sites to monitor

The next step is to register and classify the Internet addresses of selected sites, in a subject directory made up of sections and sub-sections. This directory is created in the Bookmarks file of Netscape and the Favorites file in Microsoft Explorer.

A directory of addresses for sites relating to tourism could include the following:

- DICTIONARIES: encyclopaedias, thesauruses, lexicons, glossaries etc.

- DISCUSSION GROUPS: tourism, environment, technology, forecasting etc.

- FOREIGN SITES: classified by country

- GOVERNMENTAL AND INSTITUTIONAL SITES: Parliament/Congress, Senate, Ministries, State organisations etc.

- INFORMATION SOCIETY: intelligent agents on-line, search engines, sites dedicated to Internet, statistics relating to Internet, specialised press, Internet guides and directories, directories etc.

- INTERNATIONAL ORGANISATIONS: main international organisations, international tourism organisations etc.

- LEGAL SITES

- LIBRARIES AND DOCUMENTATION CENTRES: on-line databases, libraries, market research organisations specialised in tourism, publishers of tourism guides, annual reports, theses, maps etc.

- PRESS: news and trade press, newsletters and magazines etc.

- PROFESSIONAL TOURISM ORGANISATIONS: travel, catering and hotels, transport, works committees, rural, coastline and mountain tourism, events (on-line chat rooms, organisers of seminars and colloquiums, event calendars and directories), environment (generalist sites, sustainable tourism sites, ethical tourism sites etc.), economics (statistics, forecasting, national accounting, economic, social and political outlook).

- RESEARCH AND INFORMATION: universities, research organisations, training organisations etc.

7.4.3 Automating the monitoring of sites using intelligent agents

Once the directory has been created, it is possible to select sites for regular monitoring and to set up a monitoring directory. The quantity of useful information available may turn out to be enormous, and it is necessary to organise it well in order not to be submerged. Intelligent agents, which can be programmed for sites to be surveyed, may be used to this end (keywords must be selected, search equations constructed, a hierarchy established for levels of daily, weekly or monthly monitoring). These programmes use an alert system to indicate the searches carried out and any modifications to sites found. Some intelligent agents download sites entirely, others collect all information and download databases, sectoral reports, summaries and articles etc.

It is also very useful to create an automatic monitoring system for gathering intelligence from the press. Electronic press reviews exist: the user selects press titles of interest, then sets keywords (e.g. "tourism and environment", "tourism economy" etc.) so that a daily press review is established automatically using the keywords and covering a whole set of sources.

It is recommended that the Centre subscribes to Newsletters of selected sites so that research presented on these sites may be found easily. Most sites provide free subscriptions to their Newsletters.

7.5 Collecting and organising information

Collecting information is done through selective sorting of the answers received and their subsequent classification. To do this, directories or dossiers should be created which correspond to the sections in the intelligence newsletter and information sorted into each folder. Preliminary sorting allows intelligence dossiers to be supplied from four sources of information:

- information from searches conducted on the Internet,

- information collected by email (subscriptions, newsletters, feed-back received from information networks, discussion groups etc.),

- information collected form the IDRC staff,

- internal information within the Tourism Administration.

7.6 Assessing and checking information

The intelligence gathering system is judged according to the quantity and above all the relevance of the information collected. This information must be checked, evaluated and validated. The success of Internet stems largely from its openness and free access, both for consulting and for distributing information. This makes it difficult to gauge the relevance of information. Apart from actual disinformation which some sites disseminate about their competitors, a lot of information on the Internet is not up to date, with hypertext links that no longer function. Links should therefore be checked, selected information assessed, consolidated and rendered reliable. It should then be checked by experts within the National Tourism Administration. This is important for everything connected to statistics, company reports, certain opinions expressed in articles etc.

It is recommended that a process of knowledge management is set up within the NTA so that experts may easily be found to check information.

7.7 Handling information

Information should be collected and structured in a homogenous manner, within each intelligence file. It should first be organised and structured hierarchically, and should then be summarised in such a way as to draw out the main points of interest. The sources of all information should be clearly indicated and made accessible via Internet links to the sites from which the information is drawn.

7.8 Entering information into databases

The information collected, processed and presented in the intelligence newsletter includes references to events, news etc. which may rapidly become obsolescent. Such information may be stored or archived in a directory created to this end, but is not entered into the database. Only fundamental information and documents (research work, analysis of particular subjects relating to tourism) should be entered and indexed in the three databases of the IDRC: the bibliographical database, the legal database, and the tourism professionals database. Documents which accompany the summaries entered in the databases should be digitised and linked to the bibliographical data file.

7.9 Distributing the newsletter

If the IDRC is directly responsible for distributing the newsletter, it is recommended that the emails are sent out in batches. This avoids overloading the email messaging programme, and helps preserve the mailing list so that it cannot be copied by recipients or other users of Internet. This preserves the anonymity and tranquillity of subscribers. Feed-back error messages also have to be dealt with. Lastly, each issue of the newsletter should be archived, and any feed-back (complements and comments) should be carefully stored.

7.10 A reader questionnaire

A few months after launching the intelligence newsletter, it is advisable to send out a questionnaire to its recipients to assess the contents and periodicity of the intelligence gathered, as well as the presentation of the newsletter. The mailing of the questionnaire is also an opportunity to call on readers, who hold relevant professional information, to provide information feed-back for the newsletter.

7.11 Gathering economic or competitive intelligence

Economic intelligence gathering is done in exactly the same way, though with one difference. Economic intelligence relates to competing sites (sites of competing countries) or to a specific area of tourism (e.g. seawater pollution whose impact needs to be observed). Such intelligence is used in decision-making, in formulating policy and implementing actions. Its aim is to lead to the first step in policy implementation, namely the decision on which actions to take.

ANNEX 1 A FLOW CHART FOR ORGANISING INTELLIGENCE GATHERING IN THE FIELD OF TOURISM

Sources of information collected

```
┌──────────┐   ┌──────────┐   ┌──────────┐   ┌──────────┐
│  Emails  │   │Search on │   │   IDRC   │   │   NTA    │
│ received │   │ Internet │   │ external │   │Publications│
│          │   │          │   │acquisitions│  │and grey  │
│          │   │          │   │          │   │literature│
└────┬─────┘   └────┬─────┘   └────┬─────┘   └────┬─────┘
     │              │              │              │
     ▼              ▼              ▼              ▼
┌─────────────────────────────────────────────────────────┐
│                 COLLECTING INFORMATION                  │
└─────────────────────────┬───────────────────────────────┘
                          │
                          ▼
                   ┌─────────────┐
                   │  Storing in │
                   │ a directory │
                   └─────────────┘
```

- Filtering sorting assessing
- Checking by experts
- Preparing summaries and indexing documents
- Intelligence Newsletter
- Storing in the databases

Information and Documentation Resource Centres for Tourism
© 2004 World Tourism Organization - ISBN: 92-844-0717-6

ANNEX 2 ENGLISH - FRENCH TERMINOLOGY GLOSSARY

(This glossary was created progressively as the text of this document was drafted. It indicates the choice of terms used both in English and French.)

English	French
Abstract	Résumé
Accessioning	Enregistrement
Accessioning of serials / periodicals	Bulletinage
Address file	Fichier d'adresses
Analytical bibliography	Bibliographie analytique
Assigned indexing	Indexation par thesaurus
Associative relation	Relation associative
Author catalogue	Catalogue d'auteurs
Author statement	Mention d'auteur
Automatic abstracting	Résumé automatique
Automatic indexing	Indexation automatique
Auxiliary descriptor	Mot outil
Bibliographic description, bibliographic entry	Notice bibliographique
Broader term	Terme générique
Business intelligence	Veille économique
Card catalogue	Fichier de bibliothèque (meuble)
Case file, documentary dossier	Dossier documentaire
Catalogue	Catalogue
Catalogue file	Fichier-catalogue
Catalogue record, catalogue entry (bibliographic description+shelf-mark)	Notice catalographique
Charge out	Enregistrement du prêt
Circulation desk	Comptoir de prêt
Classification system	Système de classification
Classification table, classification scheme, classification schedule	Plan de classement
Classified catalogue	Catalogue systématique
Clipping files	Dossiers de coupures de presse
Coding sheet, processing slip	Bordereau de saisie
Competitive intelligence	Veille concurrentielle
Composite author	Auteur collectif
Compound term	Terme composé
Computerisation	Informatisation
Content analysis	Analyse du contenu
Corporate author	Collectivité-auteur
Current bibliography	Bibliographie courante
Customised file	Dossier personalisé
Data bank	Banque de données
Data base	Base de données
Data entry form	Masque de saisie
Data entry, keyboarding	Saisie des données
Descriptor	Descripteur
Digitised publication	Publication numérisée
Document holdings	Fonds documentaire

Document retrieval	Recherche de documents
Documentary sequence (information system)	Chaîne documentaire
Documentary synthesis	Synthèse documentaire
Documentation centre	Centre de documentation
Documentation engineering	Ingénierie documentaire
Documentation software, documentary software	Logiciel documentaire
Economic intelligence	Veille stratégique
Electronic document management	Gestion électronique de document (GED)
Electronic magazine	Revue électronique
Electronic publishing	Edition électronique
Equivalence relation	Relation d'équivalence
Facet	Facette
File	Fichier
File card	Fiche
Filing cabinet	Armoire de classement
Full text data base	Base de données de texte intégral
Grey literature, underground literature	Littérature grise
Hierarchical language	Langage hiérarchisé
Hierarchical level	Niveau hiérarchique
Hierarchical relation	Relation hiérarchique
Hypertext markup language HTML	Langage de balisage hypertexte
Index language, indexing language, documentary language	Langage documentaire, langage de recherche
Indexing	Indexation
Indicative abstract	Résumé indicatif
Information dissemination	Diffusion de l'information
Information manager- documentalist	Documentaliste
Information processing	Traitement de l'information
Information retrieval	Recherche de l'information, recherche documentaire
Information science	Science de l'information
Informative abstract	Résumé analytique
Intelligence information manager	Veilleur documentaliste
Intelligence, intelligence gathering	Veille
International standard bibliographic description (ISBD)	Description bibliographique internationale normalisée
International standard book number ISBN	Numéro international normalisé du livre
International Standard Organisation (ISO)	Organisation internationale de normalisation
International standard serial number (ISSN)	Numéro international normalisé des publications en série
International standard technical report number (ISRN)	Numéro international normalisé des rapports
Kardex file	Fichier kardex
Keyword	Mot clé
Lexicon	Lexique
Library network	Réseau documentaire

Library science	Bibliothéconomie
Link	Lien
Loan file	Fichier de prêt
Monitoring web sites, web watching	Surveillance de site internet
Narrower term	Terme spécifique
Natural language	Langage naturel
Non-descriptor	Non-descripteur
Periodical, seria	IPériodique
Permuted list	Liste permutée
Press reviews	Revue de presse
Primary document	Document primaire
Process of analysing a document, documentary analysis,	Analyse documentaire
Rack	Présentoir
Recall notice	Avis de rappel
Related term	Terme associé
Retrieval system	Système de recherche
Retrospective bibliography	Bibliographie rétrospective
Scope note	Note d'application
Search field	Champ inversé (champ interrogeable)
Secondary document	Document secondaire
Selective abstract	Résumé sélectif
Selective bibliography	Bibliographie sélective
Selective dissemination of information (SDI)	Diffusion sélective de l'information (DSI)
Semantic field	Champ sémantique
Semantic relation	Relation sémantique
Series	Collection
Series statement	Mention de collection
Shelf list	Inventaire topographique
Shelf mark, shelf number	Cote
Shelf-mark list	Catalogue topographique
Shelf-marking	Cotation
Signaletic bibliography	Bibliographie signalétique
Sponsoring organisation	Commanditaire
Standard generalized markup language SGML	Langage normalisé de balisage généralisé
Statement of edition	Mention d'édition
Statement of responsibility	Mention de responsabilité
Structured alphabetical list	Liste alphabétique structurée
Subject catalogue	Catalogue matière (thématique)
Subject descriptor	Descripteur matière
Synonymy	Synonymie
Tertiary document	Document tertiaire
Title catalogue	Catalogue par titres
Union catalogue	Catalogue collectif
User profile	Profil de l'utilisateur

ANNEX 3 PROFESSIONAL ORGANISATIONS AND SPECIALISED PUBLISHERS

International Organization for Standardization (ISO)

http://www.iso.org

Agence française pour la normalisation (France's national organisation for standardisation) (AFNOR)

http://www.afnor.fr/

Association des professionnelles de l'information et de la documentation (France's main association of information and documentation managers) (ASBS)

http://www.adbs.fr/site/

World Tourism Organization (WTO)

http://www.world-tourism.org/

European Council of Information Associations (ECIA)

http://www.aslib.co.uk/ecia/index.httm

Records management program

http://www.archives.gov/records_management/

International Council for Scientific and Technical Information (ICSTI)

http://www.icsti.org/

European Bureau of Library, Information and Documentation Associations (EBLIDA)

http://www.eblida.org/

European Association of Information Services (EUSIDIC)

http://www.eusidic.org/

International Federation of Library Associations and Institutions (IFLA)

http://www.ifla.org/

United Nations Educational, Scientific and Cultural Organization (UNESCO)

http://www.unesco.org/

BIBLIOGRAPHY OF SUGGESTED READING AND STANDARDS

"Thesaurus del turismo e del tempo libero" prepared by Cosimo Notarstefano, Facoltà di Lingue e Litterature Straniere, Università degli Studi di Lecce, 2003

"Indicateurs de performance des bibliothèques, norme NF ISO 11620", March 2003

"Intervention de France Bouthillier lors de la conférence sur l'intelligence économique organisée au salon IDT/Net 2002", published in Bases n° 183, May 2002

"Records management, norme ISO 15-489", (April 2002)

"Actualité des langages documentaires : fondements théoriques de la recherche d'information", Jacques Maniez, ADBS 2002

"Documentation, information, connaissances : la gestion de la qualité"
Eric Sutter, Preface by Réjean Savard, ADBS 2002

"Comment rédiger une bibliographie", Arlette Boulogne, ADBS 2002

"Guide de recherche sur Internet : outils et méthodes", Béatrice Foenix-Riou, ADBS 2002

"Référentiel des métiers-types des professionnels de l'information et documentation", ADBS, 2001

"Maîtriser et pratiquer la veille stratégique", L.Hermel, AFNOR 2001

"Comment le records management peut faire progresser la transparence administrative", communication given at Lundt by Philippe Barbat, Direction des Archives de France, 2001

"Compte rendu de la conférence de Jean-Louis Levet au sein du Club Intelligence Economique", Jérôme Bondu, 15 March 2001

"Recherche d'information sur l'Internet, outils et méthodes", Jean-Pierre Lardy, ADBS 2001

"Les logiciels documentaires : description de dix systèmes de gestion du marché",
Michèle Lénart, ADBS 2001

Multilingual "Thesaurus on Tourism and Leisure Activities", WTO, 2001

"Information et documentation – Vocabulaire", ISO 5127, 2001

"Information et documentation, des métiers à redéfinir ", Michel, Jean : in : "Problèmes économiques" n° 2.690, 29 November 2000

« Manual para la creación y gestión automatizada de un centro de documentación e información turística (CDIT)", Secretaría General de Turismo de España, Instituto de Estudios Turísticos, 2000

"Documentation : recueil de normes, de règlements et de certification", AFNOR, 2000

"Comment concevoir un service web : de la théorie à la pratique", Arnaud Le Guelvouit, ADBS 1999

"Euroréférentiel I&D : référentiel des compétences des professionnels européens de l'information et documentation", European Council of Information Associations (ECIA) Guides professionnels, 1999

"Information and documentation — Bibliographic references — Part 2: Electronic documents", ISO 690-2:1997

"Records Management Program", Office of Administration, U.S. Small Business Administration, December 1998

"Information and documentation - Guidelines for the content, organization and presentation of indexes. Second edition", ISO 999:1996

« La recherche documentaire en tourisme : les outils informatisés », Hélène Bussière in : Téoros. Vol. 14 n° 3, automne 1995

"Guide pour la gestion d'un centre d'information : la maîtrise des chiffres-clés"
Bernard Chevalier, Dominique Doré, Eric Sutter, ADBS 1995

"Intelligence économique et stratégie des entreprises", Henri Martre, Documentation française 1994

"Information and documentation — Bibliographic description and references - Rules for the abbreviation of bibliographic terms", Second edition. ISO 832:1994

"Former et apprendre à s'informer", Unesco, ADBS 1993

"Les accès électroniques à l'information, état de l'offre", Jean-Pierre Lardy, ADBS 1993

"Information and documentation - International Standard Book Numbering (ISBN). Third edition", ISO 2108:1992

"Service d'information et qualité", Eric Sutter, ADBS1992

"Les marchés de l'information documentaire", Jacques Treffel, ADBS, 1991

"Guide de la gestion d'un centre d'information", Bernard Chevalier, ADBS, 1991

"Valeur et compétitivité de l'information documentaire", Jean Michel and Eric Sutter, ADBS,1991

"Documentation — Bibliographic references - Content, form and structure", ISO 690:1987

"Documentation - Guidelines for the establishment and development of monolingual thesauri. Second edition", ISO 2788:1986

"La recherche documentaire dans le contexte télématique, modalités d'automatisation et utilisation des bases de données", Michel Barès, Lavoisier 1985

« Setting Up and Running a Documentation Centre within a Travel and Tourism Administration", WTO, 1985